COFFEE

BY CHARLES & VIOLET SCHAFER

DESIGN BY ALAN WOOD

TAYLOR & NG · YERBA BUENA PRESS · SAN FRANCISCO · 1976

ISBN # 0-912738-08-1
Library of Congress
    Card #76-14182
Printed in the United States
    of America
Copyright 1976 by Charles Louis Schafer
    and Violet Schafer
Published by Yerba Buena Press,
    A Division of Taylor & Ng
400 Valley Drive
Brisbane, California 94005
    All Rights Reserved
    First Printing 1976
    Second Printing, Revised, 1977
Distributed by Random House, Inc.
and in Canada by Random House of Canada, Ltd.
ISBN # 394-73253-7

For the Pleasure of Your Company

ABOUT THE AUTHORS AND DESIGNER

For more than 25 years Charles and Violet Schafer have worked together in diverse communications fields as editors, columnists, byline writers, teachers and nationally recognized consultants in conference methods.

Their experience in looking at the world through others' eyes has influenced their practical approach to subjects. They make a special effort to answer questions before they are asked. Equally, their interest in history and folklore has given their foodcraft series for Yerba Buena Press a biographical touch.

COFFEE, the sixth in the series, has been a search into history and legends, a reason for long journeys and interviews with many coffeemen here and abroad, a purpose in collecting a library that began with the bible of coffeephiles, Uker's *All About Coffee,* and a focus for testing scores of recipes . . . all to make having a cup of coffee an experience for their readers, not just an ingestion of fluid.

Coffee's designer, Alan Wood, is a young photographer, copywriter, and packaging designer in long association with Taylor & Ng, the San Francisco retail, wholesale, and publishing firm.

A third generation Californian and a graduate of Lake Forest College in Art History, Alan Wood brings to *Coffee* a warm visual address to the role this dark brown liquid has played in history and plays everyday. With cooperation and consideration from scores of coffee lovers from around the world, he entertains the viewer with a unique and handsome pictorial collection that endeavors to suggest that special space and special time in which to enjoy, revere, and drink this special brew called coffee.

Let us talk about the Horatio Alger of the Beans which started poor and proud and ended rich and powerful.

Let us talk about the coffee bean!

Over the centuries its public appearances have attracted its share of critics of the cloth from Arabia to America. It has loosed police raids. It has brought imperial wrath down upon itself and survived.

The history of the bean, in fact, has been one, long and exciting excursion into fantastic parts of the world. It has played politics and found itself mentioned thousands of times in Spanish, Dutch, Portuguese, German, English, French, Walloon, Latin, Chinese, Arabic, Italian, Swahili, etc., etc., etc.

It caused railroads and highways to be carved out of jungles and mountain passes to ease its way to market.

It took part in marvelous adventures and swelled to praises of poets, tract writers and composers. It created favorable settings for hatching revolutions.

It had snob appeal as gifts for nobles. It had chic among the fashionable because of the pomp and ceremony of its service. It became a symbol that signaled sociability at many levels in many cultures around the world.

THE EPICAL BEAN

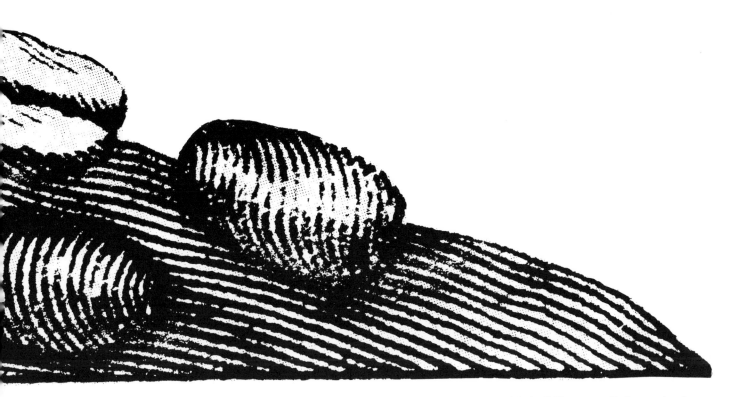

It laughed at restrictive monopolies and broke them by cunning. It endured and outlasted a myriad of persecutions. It challenged smugglers. It swaggered with extravagant claims for its powers. It decorated trademarks, placards, stamps, medals and money.

It inspired potters, silversmiths and artists to create fine coffee sets. Inventors, great and small, delighted in dreaming up hundreds of ingenious machines to better its processing, roasting, grinding and brewing. It challenged doctors and pharmacologists to plumb the secrets of its effects. It never, never met with indifference. Quite a winning fellow whose first sponsors were goats!

The bean, in truth, conquered the world. But that doesn't mean you can't make it do your bidding. You can produce a beverage with it uniquely suited to your personal taste and make it a companion of interesting foods from around the world. This book will show you many ways you can accomplish this. We hope it will also advance your reputation as a connoisseur.

Charles and Violet Schafer
Corte Madera, California

CONTENTS

THE EPICAL BEAN

THE WELL TRAVELED BEAN

The coffee bean conquered the world because it was potable, portable and profitable.

An Ethiopian of humble origin, the bean left home early in the Christian era. Before its travels were over, it settled in all the tropical lands and islands of the two hemispheres, outlasted wars and revolutions, and survived natural disasters.

BOTH MEAT AND DRINK

Coffee's special uses in its native habitat made it inevitable that the bean would travel far. Early Africans used the whole coffee plant — leaves, fruit and beans. First they ate ripe cherries. When fruiting waned, they chewed beans. They found them good.

Ancient Ethiopian warriors carried coffee balls as battle food. To this end, they rolled roasted, pulverized coffee beans in fat. One coffee ball for each man sufficed for a day's march. Its small size and stimulating character made it welcome baggage. The bean also accompanied caravans to be eaten with dates.

COFFEE AND CONQUERORS

Its departure from Ethiopia was over the Red Sea to Arabia. Possibly it was carried to Yemen by Arab slaves or African nomads or Christian Ethiopians bent on subduing Arab infidels. Some say it was the latter and that the embattled Arabs lost ground until Persian warriors joined them. As a reward for their successful intervention, the sybarite Persians requested coffee beans as booty worthy of their godlike self image.

So Persia gave impetus to the bean travels.

CULTIVATED COFFEE

However the bean arrived, Arabs had welcomed it to the ravines of Yemen and became the first coffee farmers. As early as 600 A.D. they created beverage from the bean and wine from the cherries.

Despite active trading between Arabia and the Muslims of Maghrib and the Levant, the coffee bean made slow progress, for it was not an abundant commodity. Although vague reports of its exotic taste and stimulating properties trickled from the Levant, the bean remained a curiosity. Botanists had not given it a name. It was something dispensed by apothecaries. Its rarity supported legends that coffee was a gift from heaven; that a rare songbird with exquisite plumage first led man to the coffee tree.

Travelers, learning about coffee first hand from Turks and Arabs, collected beans to take home. They jealously guarded small amounts for themselves and prized coffee as unusual gifts for friends.

A PROMISING POTABLE

The earliest cooks prepared coffee by boiling both fresh beans and whole cherries in water. They did not roast and grind beans until the 13th Century. Among the first to enjoy this innovation were the

1

Turks. They so cherished the beverage that grooms, as part of marriage ceremonies, promised always to keep their brides provided with coffee. Breaking this pledge risked divorce, for coffee was a major necessity of life.

SADDLEBAGS AND SHIPS' HOLDS

Not until the early 16th Century did Egyptians, Syrians, Persians and Turks know coffee well and open the way for the bean to hitch rides with Turkish merchants traveling between Arabia and Constantinople. There, Venetian traders discovered a fondness for the bean. They rubbed their hands over its commercial possibilities and sailed home with it to Venice. Its arrival inspired the opening of the first Venetian coffee houses in the 17th Century.

In 1644, the port city of Marseille teemed with coffee enthusiasts. The time was ripe for introducing coffee in France. Within a few years a boat from Alexandria unloaded a coffee cargo in Marseille and the first public, Levantine-style coffee houses opened.

COFFEE AND CHARISMA

The bean traveled from country to country throughout the 16th and 17th Centuries. Its major coup as a popular beverage maker was staged in noble English homes and public coffee houses. Great houses customarily provided coffee dishes and utensils for the private use of each family member. Middleclass homes could not afford the luxury.

As it became a proper English bean, the Earl of Bedford at Woburn Abbey recorded purchases of it for himself and his countess. His household accounts also listed a coffeepot, china drinking dish, and coffee set for the countess.

IMPORTANT ENOUGH TO ADVERTISE

A handbill in 1652 was the first to advertise coffee and proclaim it "quickens the spirits, and makes the heart lightsome." A newspaper ad followed in May, 1657, in the *London Public Advertiser*. It rang like a patent medicine spiel.

In Bartholomew Lane on the back side of the Old Exchange, the drink called Coffee (which is a very wholesome and Physical drink) having many excellent vertues, closes the Orifice of the Stomack, fortifies the heat within, helpeth Digestion, quickneth the Spirits, maketh the heart lightsome, is good against Eye-sores, Coughs, or Colds, Rhumes, Consumptions, Head-ach, Dropsie, Gout, Scurvie, King's Evil and many others is to be sold in the morning, and at three of the clock in the afternoon.

THE LANDLOCKED BEAN

The bean traveled more slowly in Central Europe with one exception. Coffee-loving Turks gave the bean an involuntary boost when their siege of Vienna failed. Forced to flee, they abandoned tents, animals and food. The latter included 500 sacks of

coffee beans. A soldier who had met the bean and tasted coffee in Turkey asked to carry them away. He used the opportunity to found a public coffee house.

ONE TREE — BILLIONS OF BEANS

The well-traveled bean was a humble bean no more. Still rare, however, it continued to be the darling of the privileged who could afford it.

Now the bean ceased to be a casual knapsack traveler and became cargo on scheduled voyages. A prodigious tale of coffee culture with a profit motive began to unfold. And, as we shall see, its success hinged upon beans from a single tree in its native home.

BEAN MONOPOLIES AND SNATCHES

During its first, long residence in Arabia, bean culture was a tightly regulated monopoly. To prevent its propagation elsewhere, Arabs forbade travelers, under pain of severe punishment, to leave the country with viable coffee fruits and beans. They limited exports to boiled or parched berries and beans that would not sprout. Anyone wishing coffee had to go to Mocha to fetch it.

In the end, all such efforts failed.

BELLY BEANS

What made the monopoly impossible? The bean's earliest travels and adventures suggest the answer.

They came about quite spontaneously because enthusiasts, holy and profane, burned to share the bean with others.

High destiny especially marked beans that left Mecca in 1600. This is what happened. On a pilgrimage to Mecca, Indian holy man Baba Budan tasted coffee and found it good. So he took unto himself seven viable seeds. These he bound to his belly for his return to India. Once home, he planted the seeds near Chikmagalur. From there coffee trees spread to Mysore, the Coorg and Goa; north to Berar and south to Travancore and the hills west of Tuticorin. By 1658, coffee was well established and growing profitably in India.

SEAFARING BEANS

The bean's penetration was especially rapid because of seafarers like the Dutch. Because of them, the bean moved first toward the Indian Ocean. Traditionally, Dutch ships hugged the east coast of Africa. Mocha, which gave the bean a port as well as a name, lay on their route. From there, about 1690, the Dutch carried off the first coffee stock for plantations in Ceylon and the East Indies. Java gave the bean a second name.

When the first Javanese plants matured, the Dutch took trees home to the Amsterdam Botanical Gardens. The first trees fell to the rigors of sea travel. Not until 1706 did living plants survive the long journey.

Puffed with pride at their success, authorities shared trees with other European botanical gardens. Some went to Surinam. There in 1720, despite severe restrictions, trees passed to French Guiana.

ANCESTRAL TREE

Another episode in coffee culture furthered the tale. Considering a live coffee tree a royal gift, the Dutch twice presented a tree to Louis XIV. The first tree died. The second, presented in 1713, survived and arrived in France under the care of its own exclusive attendant. The tree took up residence in the Jardin des Plantes, Paris. It enjoyed the special attention of a young curator, Antoine de Jussieu. The first glass plant house the French ever built housed it. Little was done to establish commercial culture at this time.

This royal tree was descended, they say, from Baba Budan's belly beans. In time, its seeds started billions of trees in French colonies. Coffee plantations took root by fiat of the king when colonists clamored for profitable crops to raise.

The king's tree was the progenitor of coffee trees in almost all the American tropics. From 1720 on, the coffee world expanded significantly until the New World began to supply practically all the world's coffee.

JOHNNY COFFEESEED

A very romantic episode in the spread of the bean starred French Naval officer, Gabriel Mathieu de Clieu.

Hearing that the Dutch had taken trees from Arabia to the East Indies with success, he argued that Martinique would favor coffee culture, too. So, in 1723, he sailed from Nantes on a merchant ship bound for Martinique with a few potted descendants of the king's tree. Because de Jussieu had refused to give him any plants, some say he had a band of hooded men snatch them.

A single plant arrived in Martinique in spite of storms, plantnappers, pirates, calms and awful heat.

De Clieu planted and cared for his treasure himself. First fruits came in 1726 and yielded two pounds of seeds. These he shared with friends. Their efforts founded a flourishing industry. The seeds provided a majority of the coffee plants in the Americas. By 1777, nearly 19 million trees were growing in Martinique alone. The French Antilles were covered with plantations tended by slaves and European colonists. Progress was so rapid that just before the Revolution, Martinique, Guadeloupe, Santo Domingo and Marie-Galante exported enough to supply three-fourths of Europe. This bounty contributed to the ruin of the Dutch monopoly.

The French went on to send coffee trees to what is now Haiti and Tahiti, to provide colonists with new revenue. In 1750, Spaniards took coffee to Cuba, Puerto Rico and other West Indies locations.

BEANS AND WARS AND BLOCKADES

The Revolution and Napoleonic wars made a disaster of French coffee culture. The abolition of slavery slashed manpower. Santo Domingo won its independence. The continental blockade choked off coffee shipments to Europe. Only occasional vessels escaped with contraband.

Coffee commerce came to a halt. For some reason rival shippers never exploited the situation and coffee gained new ground especially in the Americas, spreading to provinces in Brazil, Mexico and Peru.

MAKE COFFEE, NOT WAR

The French and Dutch, always the most enthusiastic coffee colonizers, also depended on descendants of that one Amsterdam hothouse specimen. The trees the French had planted in French Guiana grew but not well. Then, in 1727, an irresistible young Brazilian envoy, Francisco de Melho Palheta by changing their ecology changed their fortunes.

Ostensibly handling a boundary dispute between French and Dutch Guiana, he was secretly eyeing coffee for his emperor. Accordingly, he courted the favor of the French governor's young wife. Their friendship warmed. In a hearts-and-flowers ploy, she sent him gift bouquets with coffee seeds and viable cuttings.

Francisco sped them home to Brazil. Soon they were growing under far better conditions than their parent plants. With other introductions from Sumatra and probably Goa, they became the gold of Brazil. In later years, the shrewd Dutchman, John

Hopman, seeing its export possibilities, became Brazil's first major coffee promoter. That was two centuries ago.

BAN THE BEAN!

Although the bean's popularity kept growing in Europe, its travels were often hazardous. Critics attacked it on the pretext of preserving social, political or religious order. At times they charged that coffee was a threat to public and economic health.

An English sermon blasted tobacco and coffee:

They cannot wait until the smoke of the infernal regions surrounds them, but encompass themselves with smoke of their own accord, and drink a poison which God made black, that it might bear the adversary's color.

The Swedes made coffee illegal. Coffee raids were common. Not only could you be arrested and fined for imbibing, you could lose all your coffee cups and brewing equipment to boot.

King Gustav III, determined to find out whether coffee was good or bad for health, had tests run on a condemned murderer. He ordered that the felon drink large quantities of coffee daily. A college of physicians supervised the experiment. Authorities expected the killer to suffer a sudden, terrible death.

Years passed. Members of the supervisory college grew old and died. The sentencing judge passed away. The king himself was murdered at a fancy dress ball. Hale and hearty, the murderer outlived them all.

In the end, the ban produced more abuses than it prevented. Swedish authorities reversed themselves and returned the bean to grace.

OUT WITH THE FOREIGNER!

Germans fell to the bean craze, too. Here, the immigrant bean made the mistake of competing with entrenched beer and brandy.

While Bach praised the bean by composing his amusing "Coffee Cantata," others were less kind. Landgrave Frederic of Hesse prohibited coffee throughout his land. The disobedient drew sentences of hard labor on road gangs. Lawbreakers who could afford the indulgence without threat to their estates went unpunished.

Frederic, the Great, also attacked coffee. Coffee, he fulminated, drained money from the economy.

"Buy Prussian!" he urged. "Go back to beer! Support your domestic breweries. Beer soup is good for you!"

He said more: "Your fathers drank brandy and were brought up on beer like me. They were happy, brave people. Every pot, every fancy cup, common bowl, grinder, roaster — everything associated with coffee — should be smashed and its very memory be erased. If anyone tries to sell coffee beans, confiscate his supplies!"

Could a coffee bean overcome such odds? It could, in spite of enforcers called *Kaffeeschnüfflers*. Their mission was to sniff out illicit coffee roasters and smugglers. For their work, they collected one-fourth of the fines. Their efforts failed. The bean was too popular. The people showed their displeasure by caricaturing the repressive king and rioting. His majesty caved in.

CONTRABAND KAFFEE

Illegal commerce flourished. Coffee smugglers had a field day, showing rare gifts for high jinks, energy and originality. Well dressed smugglers wore high boots and waded up to their hips in coffee beans to fill them. They wore high hats and wide trousers in which they hid beans. When drawings of costumes appeared publicly, their cover was blown. New disguises were ordered.

A FATAL BLIGHT

The emotional, social, political and economic issues that blocked the bean's travels in Europe were harassing but dealt no death blows. That disaster waited for a Singhalese botanical blight. Although Ceylon had received its first coffee trees almost at the same time as the East Indies, their culture flowered only under the occupation of the English who succeeded the Dutch. From 1809 to 1869, production increased from a few tons to 50,000, thanks to favorable conditions and enlightened care.

By 1870 Ceylon was growing most of the world's coffee. It was the favorite beverage along Piccadilly and The Strand in London. A mere 15 years later, not a single bag left Ceylon. An insidious blight appeared and ravaged plantations. Too late, planters became alarmed. By the end of the century, the last coffee trees were gone and the blight had contaminated all the coffee growing countries in the Indian Ocean. Culture became too onerous to continue.

BRAZILIAN STAMPEDE

Brazil has dominated recent history of the bean. Until 1850, the economy of the area relied exclusively on sugar cane and slave labor. With the abolition of slavery, cane plantations collapsed. Coffee culture moved into the breach and spread rapidly. More than a million immigrants, chiefly Italians, arrived and profoundly affected coffee growing. They powered the large plantations by entering into sharecropping agreements. Immense stretches of virgin land and a favorable climate assured Brazil's success as a top world producer.

ENTER A WILD COMPETITOR

Few natural calamities troubled coffee in Brazil. Brazil could have continued undisputed monopoly of *Coffea arabica* had not new developments taken place in coffee culture.

As early as 1716, a wild coffee tree was known to grow on islands off East Africa. The bean of this

Coffea Mauritiana was bitter, devoid of caffeine and appeared to have little economic value.

A further canvass of African forests at the beginning of the present era led to discoveries of coffee trees of the *canephora* and *liberica* groups. They excited great economic interest for they will grow on the plains and lowlands of intertropical regions where *arabica* will not. From this time, the Brazilian coffee market had to look to its laurels.

BEAN MAKES GOOD IN HOME TERRITORY

By the middle of this century, the bean became a commercial success in its native Africa. Kenyan and Tanzanian *arabicas* are among the best in the world. In 1975, African coffee represented about 30 percent of the world's exportable production. Coffee is now the principal commercial crop in four African nations. More than 125 countries consume coffee.

AN ASTONISHING RECORD

The bean's major travels consumed 200 years, its greatest activity taking place in the 18th Century. All this time, coffee remained pure of lineage, no matter where it traveled.

Incredible as it seems, experts say it is very likely that a handful of seeds from a single tree was the source of today's commercial coffee.

One self-pollinating tree, growing naturally from seed, broadcast its treasure across the world — a truly astonishing record for a single crop!

TALES & TESTIMONIES

The story of coffee is a bewitching melange of fables and facts. It has attracted eccentrics as well as sober researchers with its magic and methods. Its history is tangled with missionaries, merchant travelers, colonists, starry-eyed planters, world navigators, ex-army officers, kings, queens and African tribesmen — in short, a cast of thousands! Its character and influence affect daily rituals and customs in every strata of society all over the world.

Earliest Egyptians, Greeks and Romans knew it not, or if they did, they did not tell. Abyssinians, when they recorded its use in the 15th Century, had known it from time immemorial.

MIRACLES AND LEGENDS

As the bean moved out into the world, rich tales and testimonies embroidered its going. There was the old man from Aden who wanted to ease his entrance to paradise and chewed coffee beans he had kept as curiosities. Behold! they made him whole again!

And there is a fascinating tale that gives coffee the stamp of religious approval. Some say a sad-eyed Mohammedan priest spread the gospel of coffee. Like the sleepy Buddhist saint who discovered tea, the priest fell asleep during prayers. And like the saint, he overcame his sin by discovering a stimulater.

A local prophet recommended he drink a beverage made with cahave fruit. "It has a wakeful effect on goats that eat the fruit," said the prophet. "Perhaps it can help you."

So the priest brewed cahave berries and drank. His eyes did not close that night. So impressive was the eye opener that he took fruit to the city and proclaimed its powers.

COMFORT FOR AN EXILE

Others give credit to Dervish Hadji Omer. Banished from Mocha, he fled to the hills where he discovered coffee beans. First he ate them from the tree. Too bitter! Then he roasted them. Too hard! Finally he did what primitive man has always done with hard things: he softened the beans in water. The water turned brown. He drank of it and pronounced it good.

FIRST, A PRAYING MAN'S DRINK

Whoever discovered coffee, Arabs deserve credit for coffee culture and for popularizing the beverage.

Mohammedans who embraced coffee in semi-religious ceremonies allowed only men to prepare it. They made a ritual of it and poured coffee on the fire as an offering to Mohammed.

THEN A PLAYING MAN'S SWEET

Soon coffee was secularized and became generally available. In 1500, public houses of Mecca and Medina offered music and backgammon as well as

11

coffee. Authorities watched with growing alarm as patrons disturbed the peace with loud laughter and tambourines.

Holy sanctions for coffee were withdrawn following a drinking incident in the sacred area of the Ka'bah. The Mameluk governor of Mecca appointed a Commission on Coffee to abate the nuisance and decide whether coffee's use should be permitted. For seven days, judges and academicians from Mecca, Cairo and Damascus pondered how to classify coffee. Was it a stimulant? Was it an intoxicant? Government officials, doctors and private citizens testified.

Results were mixed. There was a majority and a minority report. Numerous popular articles followed, ranging from *The Misstep and Error of Those Using Coffee* to *Rebutting the Claim of the Harm in Coffee.* Conservatives won. Coffee was banned. A precedent was set for Egypt and Syria in the years that followed.

INCOMPLETE BLACKOUT

Public censure never quite halted private indulgence. When coffee drinking was banned again in Cairo in 1532, theologians of al-Azhar issued decrees permitting its use. Its pronouncements were incontestable, for al-Azhar was as important to the Muslim as the Synod of Canterbury, Oxford University, the Houses of Parliament, Westminster Abbey and Piccadilly Circus are to the English today. The coffee decree is still remembered as a momentous one for Muslims everywhere.

In Constantinople, orthodox Mohammedans condemned coffee, too, when coffee houses filled up to the neglect of the mosques. Everyone patronized them — poets, writers, professors, scholars and civil servants. In jest, they were called "schools of knowl-edge." They were no joking matter to authorities.

"Coffee is an intoxicant," irate imams pointed out. "Surely the Koran frowns on it."

This time, dervishes and monks prepared a treatise for the mufti. They claimed that roasted beans were charcoal and so forbidden by the Koran. The mufti agreed that coffee drinking broke Mohammed's laws. Authorities locked the coffee houses.

But people drank on. As more and more embraced the fad without ill effects, authorities relaxed. They allowed coffee to be sold and drunk provided such activities were out of sight or carried on in back rooms. The government levied a luxury tax of two gold pieces a day on all places selling coffee and realized a tidy revenue. A new mufti came to power and decreed that roasted beans were not charcoal and coffee became inseparably linked with the Middle East.

MONEY AND INSPIRATION

Coffee came to mean many things to many people. Coffee beans were money in early Africa and still serve that function in isolated areas. It also served as currency in 18th Century Arabia where pashas assigned a specific number of beans for each asper.

Coffee has shaped the art of Ugandan basketmakers who weave containers for "chewing" coffee. Craftsmen in Somaliland have created beautiful wooden mortars for grinding coffee beans. Potters and silversmiths have made a fine art of coffee service. Inventors have paid their highest compliments to the beverage by dreaming up hundreds of ingenious machines for brewing.

A TRIO OF FAMOUS IMBIBERS

The roster of confirmed coffee drinkers includes persons of great distinction and widely different talents. Three eminent men come to mind.

In 1495, Albrecht Dürer on his way to Italy found himself penniless in Switzerland. To earn coffee and cake money, he cut decorative outlines for the title page of a book of sermons by St. Augustine.

William Harvey, famous for discovering blood circulation, habitually drank coffee before it was the fashion. "This little bean," he said, "is the source of happiness and wit." On his death in 1657, his will left

56 pounds of coffee to the London College of Physicians. While it lasted, it was to be brewed once a month for the pleasure of surviving friends.

Beethoven liked strong coffee. He personally counted off 60 beans for each cup — the amount equivalent to two tablespoons. We have no idea how many 60-bean cups he drank each day but it sounds average by today's standards.

GALLIC FLARE

The French have provided many lively, outrageous and devilishly clever tales as befits a nation of dedicated coffee drinkers.

A twice told tale features Fontenelle or Voltaire, whichever you prefer. Let us say Fontenelle. He loved coffee and drank it with every meal. One day, a doctor warned him that it was slow poison and would end by affecting him badly.

"I agree," replied the French academician. "For 80 years I have been drinking coffee. It must indeed be slow in its effect for I am not dead yet!"

DOUBLE ENTENDRE

Napoleon I doted on coffee. At the height of his successful continental blockade, he entered a village where the aroma of forbidden coffee filled the air. Curious about its source, he found a curé tranquilly turning a coffee roaster.

"Ah ha! monsieur le curé," said the emperor. "Tell me just what you are doing."

"You can see for yourself," replied the curé coolly. "I am doing what your majesty does. I am roasting colonial products!"

THE FEMININE TOUCH

French ladies also contributed to coffee legends. The mistress and confidante of Louis XV, Madame de Pompadour, affected a stylish Arabian atmosphere at coffee-time. It pleased her to scatter luxurious silk pillows about and have a Nubian maid serve from ornate Arabian coffee sets.

As a special homage to coffee and feminine charms, the French court drank from cups modeled after Marie Antoinette's bosom.

AWASH WITH COFFEE

King of French coffeephiles, Balzac retired at 6 p.m. and rose at midnight to work for the next 12 hours. He fortified himself with strong coffee prepared to his own recipe. He found only certain coffees to his liking and often spent hours buying the right kind. He drank 20 or 30 cups a day to the day he died, perhaps 50,000 cups during his lifetime.

How did coffee affect him? "Hardly have I drunk coffee when everything falls into place," he wrote. "Thoughts come flooding like battalions of a great army on the battlefield."

Voltaire was also a prodigious coffee drinker and was said to drink about 72 cups a day. Napoleon believed coffee did wonders for him. Drunk dark and rich, he said, coffee made him alert and fired him with energy and unusual strength for his tasks.

Other notable coffeephiles were Flaubert, Hugo, Baudelaire, de Kock, Gautier, de Musset, Zola, Coppée, Bernhardt, de Maupassant, and George Sand.

PRIDE GOETH BEFORE A FALL

The Dutch, too, enjoyed coffee. Not every Dutch housewife, however, knew what to do with coffee beans.

Early in the 17th Century, an Amsterdam merchant, hoping to spur some commercial activity, sent a gift of coffee to a business associate in Merseburg. "This is coffee which is very popular in Amsterdam," he wrote. "Have your wife grind the beans and cook them in water. Please tell me how you like it."

The Merseburger handed letter and beans to his wife.

"If an Amsterdamer thinks a Merseburger has nothing better than water to cook with, he's mistaken," huffed the lady.

So she cooked the beans in a fine meat broth and served the soup to her husband and servants. All fell ill. The Merseburger was forced to spend 16 groschen for purgatives. He did not thank his associate.

After business broke off, the Amsterdamer snapped, "I have had only rudeness for my generosity. I had five bales of coffee sent from Leipzig. All who drank beverage made from that coffee praised it. I hardly need more proof they have better taste than Merseburgers!"

GROUNDS FOR TELLING FORTUNES

In 18th Century England coffee grounds rivaled tea leaves for telling fortunes. Lovesick maidens like Arabella Whimsey had their coffee cups read. "I am in love with a very clever Londoner," she confessed. "As I want to know whether it is my fortune to have him, I have tried all the tricks I can hear of for that purpose. I have seen him several times in coffee grounds with a sword by his side."

A contemporary magazine described ladies hanging on every word of a lady's maid as she read their coffee cups. They believed she could predict their future by looking at the grounds.

TASSENFRAUEN — CUP WOMEN

Disreputable old hags plied the same trade in Germany. Belief that coffee grounds revealed the future kept an army of them alive and led to restrictive laws.

Before they told fortunes, *Tassenfrauen* expected to have a few cups of coffee to sharpen their wits. Then they filled their subject's cup half full of thick coffee and entertained with a dumb show of rascally grimaces. They turned the cup over on a saucer, turned it three times to settle the grounds and raised the cup high. Peering in crazily, they read messages of fear and hope in the grounds.

EVEN TODAY COFFEE TELLS ALL!

In much the same way, people in Greece tell fortunes by reading patterns in coffee grounds. Widely spaced grounds mean a long trip; small spacing, a shorter trip. A big blob is money, little blobs, trouble. For more than that, consult Greek gypsies.

SIGNIFICANCE OF ANOTHER SORT

In Kathryn Forbe's *Mama's Bank Account*, a cup of coffee assumes exquisite importance.

For graduation, young Katrin campaigned for a pink celluloid dresser set from Schiller's drugstore, scorning an heirloom brooch from Mama. To please Katrin, Mama sorrowfully traded the brooch for the set. Learning of her mother's sacrifice and full of remorse, Katrin took the set back and retrieved the brooch.

Returning home, she found her father in the kitchen having coffee. Katrin had never had coffee, even with milk in it. Coffee was for grownups. But father acknowledged Katrin's mature behavior by pouring a cup of coffee and saying, "For my grownup daughter."

Katrin sat very straight on her chair and drank her first cup of coffee.

COFFEE BREAK INSTITUTION

The coffee break is a special fixture in our culture. Some say it originated at sea to warm up sailors before going on watch. Others say the custom became entrenched during and after World War II. Certainly, the institution is now virtually indestructible. It even has a formally defined time frame: it lasts ten minutes to a half hour.

For a long time, the business community has acknowledged its usefulness. It perks up staffs and increases work output. It appears to be among workers' inalienable rights and is written into union contracts.

SAFETY VALVE AND MORALE BUILDER

A Public Health doctor recommends coffee breaks.

When you join others for coffee, you exchange experiences and lessen tensions. You practice skills in meeting people, firm up your ego strengths, boost your prestige and create new cores of interest. The coffee break is the town meeting brought up to date and dressed in work clothes. It represents a lone form of democracy in the culture of bigness.

According to the doctor, the coffee break setting also reduces pressures to a desirable level. Others believe coffee breaks improve morale, lower accident rates and eliminate fatigue. Rumors and grapevine talk spice coffee breaks. The resulting group thinking sometimes stimulates changes in company policy. It is said that in terms of getting things done, one coffee break is worth more than 15 memos.

ENERGY CRISIS COFFEE

Efficiency experts surveying a large industrial company took an interest in coffee breaks when they learned that 25 managers never had coffee in the company lounge.

The reason was simple: it was a status symbol for them to have private electric coffeepots plugged in and hot all day. Management called a halt to this excessive use of power.

Still the practice continued. Managers justified non-compliance, saying they liked to have coffee for clients. Besides, they said, it saved time. They didn't have to walk to and from the lounge!

COFFEE OUTRANKS TEA

Writing of military customs, Vance Packard noted protocol for obligatory affairs. When both coffee and tea are poured, the officer's wife who pours coffee must outrank the wife who pours tea. This practice probably originated in England where coffee has a higher status than tea.

LEGISLATIVE COFFEE BREAKS

Politicians in Tallahassee were once criticized for having a "big coffee break." The 48-member senate drank $1428 worth of coffee while the 119-member house drank only $43 worth in 1972 according to an audit of the state legislature. Perhaps they took their cue from Alexander Pope who rhymed that coffee makes the politician wise and see through all things with half shut eyes.

THE SOCIOLOGISTS' COFFEES

Good sense comes through in sociological research devoted to coffee breaks. Sociologists seem to agree with Sydney Smith who said, "If you want to improve your understanding, drink coffee."

The American Sociological Association schedules coffee round tables at national conferences for groups of ten who want to discuss topics with others who share their interests. The association feels that the introduction of these relaxed sessions is among its most successful innovations in conference programming.

WHAT SOCIOLOGISTS LEARNED

What have they learned about coffee breaks? Rules, manners and practices governing coffee breaks are complex. A coffee break significantly influences group sociability and morale.

WHERE TO SIT

People entering a coffee lounge have about two seconds to decide where to sit. In this irrevocable decision, they have to settle whether to sit with secretaries, supervisors, their own group or what. The higher their status, the less freedom. Those with most authority sit alone or stay away. Unless a person is female or holds high rank, it takes courage to start a new table.

SIGNS AND SYMBOLS OF SOCIABILITY

Every time one enters a new group, the offer of coffee is a significant bid. It says, "Let's talk!" It is positive in nature. If you go to a man's office and he offers coffee, it means he likes you. If he doesn't offer coffee, he may be saying he doesn't even want to talk.

STATUS AND INVITATIONS

Status is involved in coffee breaks. The military solved the problem by having officers' clubs separate from enlisted men's clubs. Elsewhere there are unwritten rules. In a college coffee shop, lady professors sit one place; secretaries, another.

Social boundaries and behavior patterns differ by regions. At the University of California, Berkeley, you are rarely introduced. You simply join a conversational group and start participating. At Harvard, you must be invited or introduced. You can't simply move in and start talking. You wait to be

introduced or say something about yourself, then enter the group.

RITUALS AND AMIABILITY

Coffee breaks are very ritualistic. They signal sociability at various levels. Talk is not transaction bound. There is no agenda, no demand that participants reach conclusions or act. Little is at stake, nothing is fateful. All can interact freely. The break is welcomed as a time when routine is interrupted in a socially acceptable way. You can leave conversations easily because everyone understands they have only transient quality.

HIGH ORDER TYNDALL SPECTRUM

All the social significance of the coffee break makes you wonder whether it's possible to enjoy a private cup of coffee. You certainly can! Did you know you can see something amazing in a cup of black coffee?

Heat coffee to boiling, fill a cup to the brim and hold it so that a light is parallel to the surface. Use the rising sun, if you like, or a flashlight.

On the surface you will see an irregular pattern of cells. These are Bénard cells first observed by Henri Bénard in 1900. They appear when the top of a liquid is cooler than the bottom.

Now, if you look at the surface of the coffee from an angle close to the axis of the illumination source, you will see beautiful colors. This is the high-order Tyndall spectrum, the very same that produces colors you see in the sun's corona, in sunrises and sunsets.

But the coffee cools and the beauty departs. Still, you can never say again that there is no beauty in a cup of hot black coffee!

COFFEE, MEN & MANNERS

Coffee had an astonishing impact on men, manners, morals and eventually commerce. It occupied a special niche in literature and life.

Early coffee houses were bachelors' paradises. Without interruption from womenfolk, a man could test his ideas, display gifts as a story teller or be entertained. Free discussion of politics there provoked extreme displeasure. Time and again church and state officials closed coffee houses everywhere in Europe and the Near East. When churchmen denounced coffee as the drink of infidels, it simply went underground.

Vintners and brewers equally opposed coffee as a threat to their interests. They lobbied for heavy taxes on the upstart drink. This attack failed, too.

In Colonial America, the coffee house never attained stature as a social institution. The general run preferred inns and taverns which dispensed ale, beer and whiskey.

MOVABLE COFFEE BREAK

The coffee house as a public institution came into being a thousand years ago in the Near East. Coffee was first available in the streets of Damascus and Cairo where vendors bearing copper vessels sold it hot in tiny cups. They went about hung from head to foot with cups and pots heated by spirit lamps. In

Neues Caffehaus

Es ist die Red
bei diesem Weib
vom Mißbrauch,
nicht vom Zeitvertreib.

time, they offered coffee from movable stalls and small carts.

Coffee was already common in the great homes of all Near Eastern cities. Homes had special coffee rooms and householders engaged coffee stewards and pages to supply and serve the beverage.

FIRST COFFEE HOUSES

With coffee widely accepted at home and in the streets, Arabians were ready to open the first public coffee houses in Mecca and Medina in 1470. The coffee habit became a distinguishing mark of a man of the world. By 1530 coffee houses with romantic names opened in Damascus. One called *Café of the Gates of Salvation* traded on coffee's vaunted capacity to inspire and inspirit without intoxicating.

By the middle of the 16th Century Constantinople had hundreds of coffee houses. An early traveler wrote of Turks drinking coffee from "little China Dishes, as hot as they can suffer it; black as Soot, and tasting not much unlike it." By the close of the century, coffee houses were common in harbor cities throughout the Mediterranean.

ORIENTAL OPULENCE AND EXCITEMENT

Near Eastern interior design and social customs set the style for both physical settings and activities of public houses as far away as France. Habitués expected luxurious cushions, lush carpets, handsome braziers and ornate metalware.

Coffee ceased to be the special property of holy men and worshippers. It was secularized. The coffee house became a male rendezvous for entertainment by singers, dancers and readers. Men talked, argued, philosophized and engaged in sedition.

TO HELL IN A LEATHER BAG

This enormously expanded activity upset sultans, churchmen and even physicians. Sultans feared public unrest. Churchmen groaned to see mosques empty. Physicians, having a proprietary interest in coffee, saw the end of a lucrative business. Authorities closed coffee houses. Wherever they found coffee, they destroyed it. Coffee drinkers caught imbibing suffered public shame. Punishments included being sewn in a leather bag and thrown into the Bosphorus.

IF YOU CAN'T LICK THEM, JOIN THEM!

All to no avail. Coffee houses reopened under greater surveillance. In Persia, wise Shah Abas, alarmed by the number of coffee drinkers who were neglecting their affairs, chose to educate. He commanded a mullah to appear daily at an establishment in Ispahan. There he conversed with early morning patrons about law, history and poetry. Having performed his mission, he bade his audience to tend to their businesses. They complied.

BANNED IN TURKEY

When it was discovered that Turks combined pleasure and entertainment with coffee, officials banned coffee houses and coffee drinking. This led to speakeasies. The prohibition was lifted. Coffee houses sprang up by the thousands and the Turks spent more on coffee than ever the French spent on wine.

LEMONADE AND . . . .

When coffee arrived in Venice, Venetian lemonade vendors added it to their line. Like Muslims, Christians cursed coffee — an invention of the devil, they charged, enough to make a man lose his soul!

Attracted by the furor, Pope Clement VIII decided to try coffee. Having done so, he declared its aroma too pleasant to be the work of satan. He baptized it, made it a Christian drink. Coffee flourished.

COFFEE IN THE STREETS OF PARIS

By the end of the 17th Century, the rage for coffee encouraged coffee vendors from the Near East to emigrate to France to set up shop. The Armenian Pascal became the first in Paris in 1672. He had a tent at the Fair of St. Germain and sent his imported Turkish waiters into the streets to sell. Hung with pots heated by spirit lamps, they offered almond and honey nougats and other Oriental sweets as well.

On cold mornings Frenchmen eagerly anticipated the aroma of Pascal's *petit noir*. No householder dreamed he could brew coffee in his own home.

Next, Pascal opened a small coffee house under the sign *Maison de Caova*. It faithfully copied cafés in Constantinople. Curious about everything Turkish, Parisians flocked in. For three sous, they could stare at the surroundings and taste a beverage only the nobility had enjoyed before.

Pascal left for London and others took his place, among them Candiol. He was the first to fill cups householders held out to him along his way. Thus coffee passed over the thresholds of French homes.

ENTER A WILY PROMOTER

What was the impetus for the spread of coffee? In 1669, the average man drank only water, home brew, apple and pear ciders, milk or grape juice. Coffee was for high society. Everyone heard about coffee but few could afford it.

Paris was a party town. Affair after affair took place, each more brilliant than the last. Then Soliman Aga, ambassador of Sultan Mohamed IV of Turkey to the court of Louis XIV, arrived. Coffee had a perfect showman. Whenever he entertained, he dramatized coffee. Huge black slaves with colorful turbans and exotic sky blue robes knelt to serve it. The coffee came in exquisite eggshell porcelain cups on gold and silver saucers laid with embroidered silk doilies. The utter novelty delighted the stylish French.

23

Soliman rejoiced. After all, coffee buoyed spirits, loosed tongues and told him what he wanted to know. The drink was soon known all over Paris as café. Molière inveighed against the snobbish Turkish ceremonies that accompanied it. Madame de Sévigné sniffed that the fad wouldn't last.

EVERYONE'S DRINK

She was wrong, of course. Time had come for coffee houses. In 1686, the Sicilian Procopio dei Costelli opened his café at 13 Rue de l'Ancienne-Comédie facing the Théâtre-Français. Paris had its first truly French coffee house — elegant, spacious, amusing, luxuriously appointed with mirrors, chandeliers and marble tables.

The café is still there with the same facade — a little run down but a classified monument. We had the pleasure of dining there with friends on a September day in 1974. It was like being in the center of an old Daumier print. It still attracts an urbane crowd and seats 250. Its exciting history is to be found in archives of France's lovely Bibliothèque Nationale.

Licensed to sell spices, ices, barley water, lemonade, milk and coffee, the early Procope's enjoyed a wide reputation for its excellent coffee, chocolate, liqueurs, ice creams, sherbets, pastries and fruit.

WOMEN'S LIBERATION

Like most early Parisian coffee houses, Procope's was closed to women. Some places allowed men to bring women guests. A few received unescorted women in segregated parlors for coffee but not hard liquor.

Denied access to these popular resorts, Parisiennes would arrive in coaches, halt them in the street in front of Procope's and order coffee. Men friends rushed out to join them and created traffic jams in the narrow street.

The great love of Voltaire's life decided to end discrimination. Dressed in men's clothes, she entered a coffee house — not Procope's. Because she was beautiful and very popular, she won her point even with Procope.

A PLACE TO BE SEEN

Frequenters wanted to be seen, to talk and to listen. Procope's attracted the geniuses of French literature and the best thinkers of the day. Because newspapers were rare, Procope's became the seat of literary criticism, the opening wedge to success or failure. Critics and playwrights often covered dramatic performances of the Comédie without even leaving the front room of Procope's. Acoustics were excellent and they heard everything at the theatre across the street.

Voltaire, Diderot, Rousseau, Fontenelle, Hugo, Beaumarchais and Zola all came for coffee, sherbet, fierce debate and interpretations of the new liberal philosophy. Procope's attracted the Encyclopedists and Ben Franklin. Robespierre, Danton and Marat rendezvoused there. Napoleon, in lieu of money, left his hat for security.

Spies infiltrated, hoping to report seditious talk to the king. The king heard enough to close the coffee houses. When that was of no avail, he taxed brewing. But the ingenious French found ways to escape his taxes.

By 1720, Paris was one big café to hear Voltaire
tell it. There were 380 garden and sidewalk cafés. In
the following 150 years, there were 3,000. Coffee
became the national beverage. It was a rare French
home that did not serve it daily.

AN INVOLUNTARY INTRODUCTION

The Austrians had a romantic introduction to
coffee and the coffee house. When Turks laid siege
to Vienna in 1683, Franz Kolschitzky, a Polish officer
familiar with Turkish, saved the city by spying
behind Turkish lines. When the siege was lifted, his
reward was 500 sacks of coffee beans abandoned by
the Turks. He became the city's first door-to-door
coffeeman. It is to his credit that he devised many
recipes to make the exotic beans appealing. He also
invented a way to filter out coffee grounds. He
added milk, served his beverage with sugar and
cream and called it Viennese coffee. It became
famous all over the world under that name.

A MAJOR HISTORICAL CONTRIBUTION

While the English coffee house was neither
elegant nor luxurious like predecessors, it brought
the institution to full flower as a powerful influence.
In their heyday, English coffee houses served many
uses. They were assemblies for all classes —
merchants, men of fashion, literary men, students
and barristers. They gave leaders their first speaking
platform. They furthered trade.

FIRST ENGLISH COFFEE HOUSE

The first English coffee house came into existence in 1652. A broadsheet in the British Museum carried the first advertisement for coffee:

Vertue of the COFFEE Drink First publiquely made and sold in England . . . in St. Michael's Alley in Cornhill by Pasqua Rosee at the Signe of his own Head.

In 1952, Sir Leslie Royce, Lord Mayor of London, unveiled a plaque to mark the tricentennial of the opening of Pasqua Rosee's. It was affixed to the wall of the Jamaica Wine House where you can still enjoy a cup of Blue Mountain coffee, if you like.

From 1652, coffee houses flourished. By 1660 they were well established with wonderful names like *Adam and Eve, Alice's, Angel, Boodles, Bunch of Grapes, Coffee Mill and Sugar Loafe, Dog,* and *Folly on the Thames.*

GOOD NEWS AND BAD NEWS

Charles II thought it urgent to suppress early coffee houses. Frequenters of these places, his proclamation read, "devise and spread abroad divers false, malicious and scandalous reports to the defamation of His Majesty's government, and to the disturbance of the peace and quiet of the nation."

Their number increased. Whatever their faults, they were vital to the scene. London's great thorofares for coaches, carts, horses and foot traffic burgeoned with shopkeepers, woolen and linen drapers, grocers, sadlers, upholsterers and book sellers. This great resort of people needed refreshment. Coffee houses filled the need. Ordinary people flocked there to try the new drink they had heard about. Congenial company and stimulation of the coffee kept them coming. Great men also consorted there and influenced the arts, science, literature and politics of the day.

WHAT COFFEE HOUSES WERE LIKE

English coffee houses were not glamorous or overly clean or even well appointed. One gasped for air, they were so thick with tobacco smoke.

Coffee was an Oriental novelty. Coffee houses were the place to enjoy it. You drank from dishes and bowls, not cups. Coffee was usually served black but you could have it with cinnamon, cloves, spearmint, sugar, sour cream, molasses or mustard. Sometimes brandy or an egg ennobled it.

Proprietors were retired soldiers, "imported" Armenians and Greeks, coachmen, barbers and women. They became agents, friends and sources of social information for patrons. They were city directories. Their establishments were homes away from home. Each coffee house had a following. Men who went to one did not frequent others.

HOUSE RULES

Some coffee houses posted rules of conduct. Proprietors promised equal treatment for all regardless of station in life. They levied fines for swearing or quarreling. They discouraged loudness and disturbances. They banned talk of religion and bad mouthing the government. The latter rule was self-serving: all coffee houses were licensed and under government surveillance.

Because gambling was an ingrained vice of the times, some proprietors forbade cards, dice, games, and betting more than five shillings. Others literally provided gambling dens, catering to all the sharpers.

THINKING MAN'S DRINK

Coffee houses thrived near centers of learning. At these "penny universities," customers entered and tossed a penny on the counter. This allowed them to read newspapers lying about and to listen to any great man present — Congreve, Addison, Steele or Pope. Talk ranged from gossip and drama to politics and law. Men spoke out on the issues of the day. An added two pence bought a cup of coffee. Some houses provided other refreshment, too. At Spencer's Breakfasting Houses, every morning except Sunday, you could have sugar, bread, butter and milk with coffee.

WHAT'S NEW?

Coffee houses were news centers. Men began their days there reading the latest gazettes. Publishers were glad to have their papers "lye for common chatt and entertainment in every coffee house board."

Patrons looked to coffee house pundits for guidance. Addison noted in the *Spectator,* April 26, 1711:

I, who am at the coffee-house at six in the morning, know that my friend Beaver, the haberdasher, has a levee of more undissembled friends and admirers than most of the courtiers or generals of Great Britain. Every man about him has, perhaps, a newspaper in his hand, but none can pretend to guess what step will be taken in any one court of Europe till Mr. Beaver has thrown down his paper, and declares what measures the allies must enter into upon this new posture of affairs.

A PLACE TO DEBATE

Coffee houses were hot beds for political discussions and impromptu seminars. Times were ripe for testing ideas and the coffee houses gave many a man a place to hear and be heard.

"I appear on Sunday nights at St. James's Coffee-House, and sometimes join the little Committee of Politicks in the Inner-Room, as one who comes there to hear and improve," observed Addison.

Sometimes debaters, after lively discussion, put opinions to the vote. No wonder that an English coffee house contributed the world's first ballot box.

GENERAL STORE

The coffee house was marriage bureau, lost-and-found headquarters, and a place of general business. One could, if he were a Colly Cibber, rent a stage costume at the coffee house.

CLUBHOUSE

At times, the coffee house was a man's club.

The coffee-house, wrote Addison, is the place of rendezvous to all that live near it, who are thus turned to relish calm and ordinary life.

It is very natural for a man who is not turned for mirthful meetings of men, or assemblies of the fair sex, to delight in that sort of conversation which we find in coffee-houses. Here a man of my temper is in his element; for, if he cannot talk, he can still be more agreeable to his company, as well as pleased in himself, in being only a hearer.

Feminine charm was not absent. A pretty coquette tended bar at a coffee house near the Temple.

. . . a piece of furniture almost as necessary for a coffee-room . . . as the newspapers. This lady . . . has

many admirers glad of an opportunity to relieve themselves from the severe study of the law by a soft conversation with this fair one, and repeating on the occasion all the tender things they can remember from plays . . .

EARLY POST OFFICE

Coffee houses provided mail service. In the late 17th Century William Dockwra operated a Penny Post in Mr. Barker's Coffee House; and Robert Murray, one in Mrs. Hannah's Coffee House.

A magnificent oversized volume, *The History and Survey of London from Its Foundation to the Present Time, 1756* reports that a "Penny-Post Office was projected by David Murray, an Upholder in Pater-Noster-row, in 1683, who communicating the same to William Dockwra, he carried it on for some Time with great Success; till the Government laid claim to the same as a Royal Prerogative; which Dockwra being obliged to submit to, had, in return, a Pension of two hundred Pounds *per Annum* granted him by the King during Life."

Coffee houses collected mail on holy days even after the government suppressed the Penny Post. Men continued to use coffee house addresses for mail responding to ads they placed in papers.

GROCERY

Some coffee houses offered ground coffee for do-it-yourselfers. According to *Mercurius Publicus,* March, 1662, the Coffee House in Exchange Alley retailed

the right coffee-powder, from four shillings to six shillings per pound, as in goodness; that pounded in a mortar at three shillings per pound; also that termed the right Turkie Berry, well garbled, at three shillings per pound – the ungarbled for less; that termed the East India Berry at twenty pence per pound, with directions gratis how to make and use the same.

A BUSINESS PLACE

The coffee house was a place where a man could drive a bargain and get information needed to carry on business.

Lloyd's Coffee House was such a place. Originally it was a loose association of merchants who did business with each other and gossiped at Lloyd's in Tower Street, London. First notice of it appeared in the *London Gazette,* February 18, 1688. Lloyd had a coffee house near the Thames and kept tabs on ship movements and other mercantile matters. Patrons were merchants connected with the sea.

Present day Lloyd's of London is one of the world's most unusual businesses and a prestigious member of the British financial community. Its 7,700 underwriters will write a policy on everything from a killer whale to a Scotch whisky distiller's nose.

What makes Lloyd's different is that it is not even a company. It is a "society" doing business very much as it did in the 17th Century. Stationed about Lloyd's are "waiters." The title harks back to coffee house days when men waited on tables. They still wear traditional livery in order to be quickly recognized when an underwriter needs a messenger or page.

ORIGIN OF TERM "UNDERWRITER"

Lloyd's first major insurance business involved ships and their cargoes. Men willing to underwrite such insurance gathered at Lloyd's and Lloyd encouraged them by providing pens, ink, paper and shipping information.

The term "underwriting" probably originated there. Each man wrote his name and the amount of insurance he was willing to undertake at the bottom of each policy — one name under the other — until they subscribed the full amount.

THE OLD ORDER CHANGES

After two centuries, the Coffee Age was snuffed out by high taxes and tea. Coffee houses disappeared in England, not to reappear until the 1950s. Only the Viennese coffee houses continued their original form and spirit into the present.

Coffee houses in America are now more important. Like the 18th Century establishments, they are news centers. Patrons find newspapers from all over the world, paperbacks and magazines. There are chess boards, exhibits of photography and original art, musical backgrounds with hi-fi or live performances by actors, folk singers and string quartets. Poetry readings and lectures are common.

One finds them in resort areas, on campuses, in the heart of cities, on church grounds and in suburbia. Some routinize their entertainments, offering folk-singing one day, jazz the next, classical music on Sunday and poetry readings on Monday. Always there is the ferment of discussion and coffee every style. The coffee house has come full circle.

THE CONVERTIBLE BEAN

The coffee bean, like the Romans, conquered whole regions only to be converted by the conquered. Nations everywhere welcomed the bean and cloaked it in distinctive garb. Their inventiveness in converting the bean to national tastes embraced raw primitive styles as well as sophisticated methods and additives. You will find many ways appealing, not only to your taste buds but also to your sense of theatre and social grace.

STANLEY AND LIVINGSTONE EXCHANGE

We are told that Stanley on finding Dr. Livingstone asked, "Dr. Livingstone, I presume?"
To this the doctor replied, "Just in time for coffee, Stanley."

He was not thinking about sharing a beverage or bean prepared African style. Or was he?

SOUP TO NUTS

John Speke, African explorer, found people around Lake Victoria using coffee in a soup. In Central Africa, Somaliland and Ethiopia natives pick and dry young coffee cherries for chews. They also peel ripe skins off the seeds and dry them to brew a tea that tastes of straw. Ethiopian tribes still roast and grind coffee beans and mix them with fat to form small nuts. These they eat like candy for their concentrated effect.

EVERYDAY COFFEE IN AFRICA

Somalis eat roasted and ground coffee solids with toasted cereals. Where unprocessed coffee beans are available in native markets, they sell as chews.

In Ugandan village markets you can find spiced coffee fruit. To prepare them for sale, natives steep green beans in water with sweet grasses and spice herbs. They reach market carefully dried and wrapped in grass packets to hang in your house.

A WELCOME SIGN

In Arabia, the aroma of roasting coffee is everywhere. Sounds of mortar and pestle grinding beans ring like bells across the desert. Businessmen sweeten deals with demitasses. There is always time for a cup of coffee.

AHLAN WA SAHLAN

"Ahlan wa Sahlan, my home is your home," greets guest and stranger. If your host is a Bedouin, expect an elaborate ceremony as he assembles his custom-made coffee furniture from a special chest for you. He roasts fresh beans in a long-handled cast iron ladle and keeps the beans moving with a long iron stirrer. The beans cool in a shallow bowl made for the purpose.

Next, he pulverizes the beans in a brass mortar. This pounding ritual is an art full of exciting rhythms. To say "So-and-so pounds coffee from morning to night" is to say how generous a man is and how often he entertains.

When coffee is ready, the host's eldest son serves. He holds a stack of small handleless cups in the palm of his right hand and pours from a long spouted brass pot with his left. Important guests receive first. Others receive in order of seniority.

You receive and hold the half-filled cup in your right hand. Cardamom or ground ginger may flavor it. You accept one to three cups. When you wish no more, you extend your cup to the server and rotate it by moving your wrist, but not your arm. Or you say, "Khalass" or "Bass," "I'm finished; that's all." You leave and your host murmurs, "Go in God's safekeeping."

ANCIENT WELCOME MAT

It is easy in Arabia to see decision makers, even the king. They hold *majlis*, early morning open house for those with something important to say or a complaint to make. A historical meaning for *majlis* was "literary club." A thousand years ago *majlis* in private homes and rulers' courts attracted leading intellectuals to spirited literary debates on every imaginable subject. Since 1906 *Majlis* has designated the Persian National Assembly.

CAREFUL ORCHESTRATION

In Kuwait, sheiks and important merchants hold regular *majlis*. Visitors receive a round of coffee on arrival and a second cup ten minutes later. Coffee is always served in small egg-shape cups. The subtle hint to go comes with passing a scented wood in a hand censer.

A RECIPE WITH REVERENCE

Arabians drink coffee 25 or 30 times a day. This is how to make it appetizing, richly aromatic, flavorful, stimulating and never bitter.

ARABIAN COFFEE

Grind roasted mocha beans to fine powder. Never use instant coffee. It dissolves in water. Finely ground beans do not.

It is nice to have an ibrik for brewing. This long-handled, tapering brass or tin-lined copper pot comes in 2, 3, 4, and 6 cup sizes. But you can use any small open pot. Into it measure exactly 1 demitasse of cold water for each cup to be served. Bring to boil. Add 1 heaping teaspoon coffee for each cup. Stir. Let water boil up again until foam rises to top. Remove pot from fire. Cool slightly and let foam subside. Add

powdered cloves, cracked cardamom seed or pinch of cinnamon to taste and return to fire. Boil up three times.

Rinse cups by pouring a little fresh hot coffee from one cup to another. Pour this rinsing coffee on the ground to honor Coffee Saint Sheik ash-Shadhili.

Spoon creamy foam into each cup. This is "the face of the coffee" and you lose face if you serve coffee without it. Fill your guest's cup just half full, no less, for that would be insulting; no more, for that would be insulting, too.

Two cups for each guest is all. Three are for enemies, for it is said, "The first cup is for the guest; the second, for enjoyment; the third, for the sword."

A DRINK TO COMFORT THE BRAIN

Turkish coffee, said Francis Bacon, was "made of a Berry of the same name, as Black as Soot, and of a Strong Scent but not Aromatical; which they take, beaten into Powder, in Water as Hot as they can Drink it; and they take it, and sit at it in their Coffee Houses, which are like our Taverns. The Drink comforteth the Brain and Heart and helpeth Digestion."

AND REMEMBER THE GROUNDS!

You make Turkish coffee as you make Arabian except that you add sugar or honey. You eat grounds and all.

TURKISH COFFEE FOR TWO

Use a long-handled ibrik or small saucepan and Turkish grind coffee.

Measure 1½ demitasses of water into pan. Add 2 heaping teaspoons sugar and bring to boil. Stir in 1 heaping tablespoon coffee. Boil up three times. Remove from fire and add a little cold water. Serve froth first and carefully pour or spoon thick infusion into demitasses.

Allow a few minutes for the coffee to settle before you drink. Theoretically, it will, though actually not always. You may end with powder in your mouth.

RAW COFFEE POWER

A sobering experience with ground-filled, powdery coffee came for me in French Noumea. It was my first day as airline station manager and my staff was introducing me everywhere like a king. The day ended with a dinner at the finest hotel and without a word about coffee drinking or the fact that local coffee was strong enough to dissolve a spoon.

In New Caledonia, coffee beans are roasted black and ground Turkish style. The thick beverage is served with a pitcher of hot milk. Since it looked like regular coffee to me, I poured the hot milk, stirred and drank.

It went like hot lava to the back of my mouth and down my throat. My ears stung. My hair stood up. Little tremors of shock ran all over me. I winced in pain and surprise. Everyone roared with delight. It was very funny to put one over on the smart young man who had come to run the station.

I never stirred my coffee again. I let it stand and abandoned cups half full of grounds when I finished.

VARIATIONS ON THE THEME

Variations of Arabian-Turkish coffee are everywhere. Armenians, Syrians and Egyptians add powdered sugar to taste. The Lebanese serve it with condensed milk squeezed out of a tube like toothpaste. Others in the Near East flavor it with saffron, cloves or cardamom. Greeks who acquired a taste for Turkish coffee during centuries-long Turkish occupation sip it black, sweet and burning hot from thimble size cups.

Degree in sweetness of Greek coffee is up to you. *Bitter* is without sugar. *Medium* has 1 teaspoon sugar. *Sweet* has at least 2 teaspoons sugar. *Heavy sweet* preferred by men who frequent coffee houses is strong in both coffee and sugar.

GREEK COFFEE

Use 1 demitasse of water for each serving, sugar as required and 1 heaping teaspoon Turkish ground coffee. Boil up 3 times in an ibrik or small saucepan.

To serve, pour to ¼ inch of top of cup. If you are making several cups, spoon foam into each cup before you pour. Let grounds settle. Sip and eat the thick liquid.

If you start another batch, keep remains of first pot, adding water, coffee and sugar as required.

COFFEE TELLS ALL

One of the first things a Greek girl learns to make is coffee. She does the honors for guests. Where arranged marriages are customary, she may use coffee to reject a suitor provided no one loses face. She simply serves his coffee without foam. That tells all. In the same way, once married, she can warn her husband he is out of favor.

SWEETS BREAKS

Greeks drink coffee all day long. Their coffee sweets are legendary. Pastry shops have sidewalk tables for patrons who watch the world go by as they enjoy "sweets from a large pan" — almond cakes topped with honey, sugar and lemon glaze; elaborate cookies built in layers; rich chocolate cakes frosted with a sweet paste made with sesame seeds; and kataifa.

We had the delicious kataifa in a Greek coffee house in Seattle. The owner came out of his bakery at the back of the shop to tell us how to make it.

Kataifa is a delicate white wheat product that looks like raveled wool and is as hard to pull apart! You buy it in Greek pastry shops by the pound and keep it in your freezer until you are ready to use it. Phyllo pastry sheets, thin as handkershief linen, are also available in packages.

KATAIFA

5 or 6 phyllo pastry sheets
Softened butter to spread between sheets

½ pound kataifa dough
1 teaspoon cinnamon
1 cup finely chopped walnuts
¼ teaspoon ground cloves
2 or 3 tablespoons sugar
2 eggs well beaten
1 cup sweet butter, melted

Syrup: **Combine 1 cup honey, 1 cup sugar and 1½ cups water. Bring to boil in saucepan and boil 15 minutes. Add juice of half a lemon.**

Make kataifa in a cookie sheet with sides. Line pan with layers of phyllo, brushing each layer with butter. This is exacting work as sheets are very thin and tear easily. Spread half the kataifa over phyllo sheets. Combine walnuts, sugar, spices and eggs and spread evenly over kataifa. Spread remaining kataifa on top. Pour melted butter over all. Bake at 375° for 30-35 minutes or until golden brown. Pour syrup over baked kataifa as soon as it comes from the oven. Cool and serve. Cut in small squares.

Kataifa freezes well. You can cut it in small squares to serve without defrosting. Delicious!

Yield: 40-50 servings

COSTA RICAN SOCK COFFEE

In Costa Rica, the coffee roast is so dark it looks burned. A Costa Rican coffee farmer roasts only enough beans for two days ahead, using a flat pan like a wok. He lets the pan heat up and keeps stirring the beans. He grinds only enough beans for the day, grinding fine, though not as fine as Turkish coffee.

To make coffee, he uses a flannel cloth, folds it like a sock, puts in a tablespoon of coffee and pours boiling water down through the sock. This method produces very thick, strong coffee and filters out most of the grounds.

The Costa Ricans do not boil the sock to freshen it. That might spoil its flavor. They simply rinse it in cold water and hang it on the wall.

COFFEE ECONOMIES

In Colombia, people eat, drink and live coffee. Wherever you go, you talk about coffee not sports. In both Colombia and Brazil, coffee comes in small cups all day long for business and social affairs.

Since they produce more coffee than anyone else in the world, Brazilians might be considered experts. They roast beans very high, almost to carbonization, and grind very fine. They use a combination of Turkish-French brewing methods. Official receptions shun alcohol: coffee is king.

Business calls bring out cafèzinho. This is made like the "sock" coffee of Costa Rica from dark roast, finely ground coffee.

CAFÈZINHO

For each serving, bring ½ cup of water to boil in a saucepan. Put 2 level tablespoons coffee for each cup in a cloth strainer or "sock." Pour boiled water over it into preheated coffeepot. Serve sweetened with brown sugar in demitasses that have been dipped in hot water.

VIVA MEXICO!

In Mexico City coffee is very cosmopolitan. If you prefer the traditional, try *cafe de olla* made in an earthenware pot. Or simply pound roasted beans to a powder in a cloth bag and immerse bag and all in a pot of boiling milk and water.

CAFE DE OLLA

For each serving, use 1 cup water, 3 tablespoons dark roasted, coarsely ground coffee, 1 stick of cinnamon and brown sugar to taste.

First boil the water. Add remaining ingredients. Boil up twice, strain and serve.

THE VIENNESE WAY

The Viennese enjoy the best of two worlds with Turkish coffee and a coffee of their own invention. Coffee all over Vienna is very good. Perhaps this is the result of preparing it with excellent municipal tap water; perhaps it's the particular blend of coffee beans or the addition of a little Feigenkaffee, powdered figs. These are things you can explore.

You can find as many as 35 variations: coffee straight in big cups; coffee brown and gold, depending on how much milk you use; coffee melange, half milk and half coffee; coffee "upside down" with 4 parts milk to 1 part coffee; and coffee with a dollop of whipped cream or *Schlagobers*, to

name five. On warm days, you can have it iced with a scoop of vanilla ice cream topped with whipped cream.

SWEET AND SCIENTIFIC

Germans like coffee with Schlagzähne, whipped cream, vanilla ice and sometimes shaved chocolate or honey.

Typically, they have lavished their genius for scientific inquiry and efficiency on coffee. Ferdinand Runge discovered and isolated caffeine in the late 1800s. Ludwig Roselius invented a decaffeination process in 1900. By 1912 he had founded Kaffee Hag Company, predecessor of Sanka in the United States. In 1908, a frugal German housewife, Melitta Bentz, invented the forerunner of all filters in her kitchen in Dresden. Today, Germans make a neat little thing of instant coffee. It looks like bouillon cubes wrapped in waxed paper and is packed in boxes to travel. One cube to a cup of boiling water makes coffee wherever you are.

GERMANS HAD A NAME FOR IT

Coffee's first coming to Germany displaced beer for breakfast. Its wide acceptance led to the *Kaffeeklatsch* early in the 19th Century. When burgers' wives could afford coffee they began to hold coffee parties at home. These "coffee-gossips" gave women a world of their own where they talked about their homes, children, sewing and kitchens. They exchanged recipes. Their rich cookies, coffee cakes, tortes and cream puffs came to be synonymous with coffee serving.

CAFE ESPRESSO

In Italy, coffee is a motive for dramatic methods, materials and machinery. The best known coffee is *espresso*. The sheer theatricality of its machinery and vivid taste of the brew have attracted devotees in many cultures all over the world.

Italians roast very dark and grind fine. *Espresso* is about four times stronger than American coffee. It is served black with lots of sugar to cut bitterness and at times with a twist of lemon peel or a cinnamon stick.

Espresso means "squeezed out." The *espresso* machine uses live steam, about 60 pounds to the square inch, to force water at near boiling point through a finely meshed steel sieve holding coffee powder.

An equally popular drink made with *espresso* machines is *cappuccino*, black coffee mixed with an equal amount of milk steamed to a custardy froth. For this, some machines have steam injectors which can be immersed in milk. It is a very noisy business and precludes continuing any conversation in progress.

STYLISH AMBIANCE

"A cup of coffee for an old man is like a doorpost, for it supports and strengthens him," goes an old French saying. Coffee's benign presence is also evident in French children's books written about it. Frenchmen savor coffee at the end of a meal and hate to brush their teeth after breakfast coffee. American tourists who ask for water after drinking coffee puzzle waiters.

French coffee is less strong than Italian but stronger than American. Two roasts are common. *High roast* is oily, almost black and bitter. *Sugar roast* has sugar added. It carmelizes and makes beans shiny and black. Beans are ground as needed and ground finer than in America. This contributes to its strength. According to the Comité Français du Café methods of making coffee are, in order of preference, percolator, pot with filter, salam filter, and cona vacuum.

FRENCH COFFEEPOTS

The French with their genius for intricate refinements did much to improve coffee makers. De Belloy invented the French drip pot about 1800. His pot allowed boiling water to drip through ground coffee held in suspension by a perforated grid. His contributions as inventor, we like to think, caused a street to be named for him in Le Vesinet, our town in France.

FRENCH STYLE

Even the smallest things are converted to pleasure in France. As guests in a beautiful old house in Le Vesinet, we discovered this means a breakfast of *café au lait* and croissants or brioches still warm from the bakery.

The wonderful bakers by law must offer fresh bread seven days a week. They open early, close from 12:30 to 4:00 and open again from 4:00 to 7:00 or 7:30. Our baker was a short walk from the house. We left by a big wrought iron gate that opened with a huge old key and started off across one end of the town park.

Homely, familiar sounds attended our going — the crunch of our shoes on gravel paths; demanding and insistent quacking of ducks on the winding stream in the park; distant ringing of church bells in the town square; frantic barking of a dozen *chiens méchants* locked behind iron grill fences and asserting their protective role.

The baker's shop was spotless. A taciturn man with a Sigmund Freud beard, the baker wore a white smock like a doctor's. He and his assistants were busy handing out bare baguettes and sacking brioche and croissants in thin wax paper bags.

CAFÉ AU LAIT TIME

We took our warm bread and rolls and hurried home for *café au lait*. Our hostess, Mme. Sellars, had freshly ground the coffee and its fragrance clung to the air. Now it was fresh perked and ready to pour. To accompany it was hot milk in a pleasant brown earthenware pitcher. As the milk warmed on the stove, we were recruited to beat it to a froth with a whisk. We half filled our cups with hot coffee and completed the cup with hot milk. How good and sweet it was!

DEMITASSE, BLACK COFFEE AND DUCKS

During the day, the French have demitasse brewed in drip pots. For a larger serving, ask for a "double." In the evening, after dinner coffee is *café noir*, served with sugar cubes. This brings small children on the run.

"*Canard!*" they pipe. "*Canard!*" They want sugar lumps dipped halfway into the coffee. These are the "ducks," brown on the bottom with coffee and white on top like ducks in a pond. These coveted treats make a festival of serving after dinner coffee.

Not only tots like *canards*. A Swiss coffee dunk uses a *canardli*, a little duck shaped glass or silver dish. You pour kirsch into a depression, using a small silver spoon, and dip a sugar cube into the kirsch. You pop the cube into your mouth and sip black coffee through it.

In Normandy, *café arrosé avec Calvados* is a favorite. Distilled apple cider, calvados makes a jolting after dinner drink. On cold mornings, Parisian workmen like to start the day with a cup half filled with strong sweetened coffee filled to the brim with calvados. Dynamite!

DUTCH TREAT

A Dutchman in The Hague will take his coffee in an elegant place even if he has to pull in his belt the rest of the week. At least that is what jealous people in Amsterdam and neighboring towns tell you.

Coffee is probably Holland's most common drink. It comes with milk and sugar and plays a big part in the lives of the people. In the cities, Italian *espresso* is very popular.

The Dutch have hearty breakfasts with coffee rich in thick, sweet cream. They have coffee with milk between 9:00 and noon. At noon comes the *koffietafel*, coffeetable, with sandwiches or a small hot dish.

WHERE COFFEE IS KING

The Scandinavians are the champion coffee drinkers of the world. Even transplanted, they never abandon coffee. When we lived among Norwegians in the coulees of Wisconsin, we learned that coffee was not just a drink. It was an affront to reject it. It was even a social obligation to drink it every Thursday. That day Ladies Aids held coffees at church parlors in town. For a dime, we had all the coffee, sandwiches and cake we could manage. Coffee was always rich. We learned to drink it black, though never in the approved style with a lump of sugar between our teeth.

According to Hjordis Anderson of Winnipeg who toured Norway recently, some of the best coffee is made in an old fashioned pewter teakettle. Coarse ground coffee is brought to a boil in the kettle, held there for a second or two and let stand to settle. "The kettle comes right to the table and is poured," said Mrs. Anderson. "That coffee was just delicious. They call it *grug*.

"At the penjonate at Balestrand, I asked how they made coffee and was told the water was boiled in a large container, then a little cold water was put in to cut the temperature and the coffee put in. It was kept on low heat just to hold temperature and steeped ten minutes. It was also very good."

Everywhere she went, Mrs. Anderson found the flat bread, lefse. "It is not the mashed potato variety we have been used to, but a sweeter, more cake-like kind that is spread with butter and sprinkled with sugar and cut into serving pieces. Norwegians eat it for lunch, desserts, and any time they have coffee, any place!" We have found this flat bread available in many gourmet shops and departments. It is worth asking for.

Other coffee companions in Norway include sponge cake light enough to float; Mor Monsen's biscuits which are stuffed with almonds and currants, baked in sheets and cut in fancy shapes; heart shaped waffles; and linser, for which Jacob was said to have sold his birthright! Linser are custard tarts.

LINSER

2½ cups of flour
1 cup butter
4 tablespoons sugar
2 egg yolks
1 cup thick vanilla custard

Combine flour, butter, sugar and egg and let rest for two hours. Roll out dough ¼ inch thick and press into well buttered tart pans. Put 1 tablespoon custard in each pan. Roll out remaining dough to make a cover for each tart. Bake at 350° for 20 minutes.

Yield: 16 tarts

INVADING TEA TERRITORY

Coffee is popular in Taiwan. The cool, quiet, elegant coffee shops in downtown Taipei have captured two distinct clienteles — young people and businessmen. The young enjoy coffee sweetened by guitar music and American style folk singing. Businessmen take theirs with soft piano renderings of oriental songs. Cups are ornate, waitresses efficient and friendly. Evening audiences join in group singing and find the entertainment inexpensive.

Tokyo has thousands of coffee houses, too. Many Japanese have embraced them as ideal places to polish their English.

"The best way to master English is to converse freely," says one coffee shop owner. He should know. He owns a neighboring conversation school. For $1.20 his coffee customers can spend a whole day soaking up conversational English.

COFFEE DOWN UNDER

Australian coffee ranges from primitive bush variety made in a Billy can to *espresso*. The Billy is a tin bucket like the syrup buckets once used for making mud style coffee over open camp fires.

Australians once made coffee, then added milk and brought it to a boil. It was perfectly awful stuff. "Then about ten years ago," a friend told us, "instant coffee came in. That put Australians on to coffee. Now it is popular enough to replace morning tea."

COFFEE IN LONDON

Our experiences with coffee in London were very pleasant. We remember with lasting affection having coffee in the Green Man in Harrod's basement. There, in a small paneled room with a fireplace merrily alight and Persian rugs on the floor, we sat in cosy intimacy equal to any private drawingroom. The padded silence lowered conversation to a whisper and we reveled in the service on the little table. The coffee was excellent, the environment conspiratorial. Marvelous!

MR. HIGGINS, COFFEEMAN

The Higgins retail establishment at 42 South Molton Street is proof of London's sophistication in the coffee line. The original Higgins was a Mr. Tiffany sort. His shop today displays coffee like jewels. Coffee is weighed out by beautiful old brass balance scales with weights and scoops. The whole place deserves to become a shrine to coffee and common sense. Mr. Higgins, you see, challenged the idea that all coffees must be blended and sold under brand names to keep ingredients secret.

Higgins lists 27 coffees with helpful legends like this:

> Double A Chagga (*The original Mr. Higgins' greatest discovery*)
>
> *Strength and flavor are well balanced and of good quality. The Chagga coffee industry consists of more than 550 cooperative society and coffee farms affiliated to the Kilimanjaro Native Cooperative Union, Ltd. It represents one of the most advanced cooperative agricultural developments in all Africa.*

When you go to London, visit this wonderful place!

THE BIGGEST, AS USUAL!

The biggest buyers, if not biggest coffee drinkers in the world, are Americans. The United States buys half the world's coffee crop. American consumption by the pound is the highest in the world. Americans are said to drink between 500 and 680 cups a person each year.

CONDENSED PANTHER

Coffee had its share in winning the West. The American cowboy liked coffee so strong that "cowboy coffee" still has a special meaning. The brew was called "six shooter coffee," "belly wash" and "brown gargle." Cowboys drank it black, shunning milk for fear of attracting milking chores. "Canned cow" was never popular. Few ever saw sugar. If it was available, the cook couldn't keep it dry or free of ants. Those who hankered for sweetening used "lick" or molasses.

Standard coffeepots for a dozen men held three to five gallons. Lacking a pot, the cook used a kettle or metal bucket, filled it two-thirds full of water, brought it to a boil, threw in a handful of coffee for each cup and continued boiling for 30 minutes. Because water for coffee often came from ponds neither pure nor clean, boiling was very important.

When the cook thought it had boiled enough, he settled the grounds with cold water, and cowhands helped themselves. A cook's popularity depended on his keeping his coffeepot hot day and night.

Most famous suppliers of coffee to the range cow business were the Arbuckle Brothers of Pittsburgh. They were the first successfully to distribute coffee nationwide. They shipped beans already roasted and coated with sugar and egg white to keep them fresh. Coffee came in one-pound Manila bags illustrated with a flying angel wearing a red scarf. "Ariosa Coffee" read the label in bold black, cream and red. In the packages were prizes — sticks of striped peppermint or coupons which could be accumulated for alarm clocks or razors. Cowhands were lured to grinding beans with the promise of these prizes.

VIABLE CONVERSIONS

Now you have an inkling what nations have done to make an Ethiopian goatherd's discovery peculiarly their own.

The conquering bean has been perfectly assimilated. In each new environment, the same beans took on new national styles of roasting, grinding, brewing and serving. The beverage itself, whether served in thimble size cups or big mugs, became a symbol of hospitaltiy and an assurance of a stimulating pause in the day's occupation.

THE CHERRY BERRY

WHAT IS COFFEE?

What fruit product is most often used in the average American home?

Would you guess coffee? that coffee begins as the yield of an evergreen with fleshy, bright red cherries? and that we discard the cherries for their pits or beans?

EARLY BOTANICAL DESCRIPTIONS

The first Europeans described coffee late in the 16th Century. In *Plants of Egypt*, doctor-botanist Prospero Alpini related personal experiences with coffee in the bazaars of Aleppo. He included a sketch and description of a coffee tree seen in a Cairo garden.

Leonhardt Rauwolf, a widely traveled doctor from Augsburg, also observed the use of coffee in the Middle East. Muslims, he wrote, drank coffee every morning "without fear of being seen . . . in small deep earthenware or porcelain cups, as hot as they can stand it . . . only take tiny sips, passing the cup on to the person sitting next to them."

The beverage, he said, was made with water and fruit the size and color of laurel berries. Bazaars sold both beverage and berries.

At the beginning of the 18th Century, seamen from Saint Malo sailed around the Cape of Good Hope to load coffee in Arabia. They returned with stories of coffee culture in the high country of Yemen. A book describing their expedition had an exact sketch of the tree in nature.

About this time, the Amsterdam conservatory received from Java a coffee tree descended from an earlier introduction from Yemen. At first the tree excited little interest among botanists although Curator de Jussieu inaccurately designated it *Jasminum Arabicum*.

When Linnaeus studied the tree later, he corrected the name. It was not a jasmine. He named it *Coffea* in his *Genera Plantarum* published in 1737. His description in *Species Plantarum* still obtains for *Coffea arabica*.

NATIVE TO ETHIOPIA AND AFRICA

Coffee grew spontaneously in the high Ethiopian plateau, notably along Lake Tana. It also grew around Victoria Nyanza, in Angola, the Congo Basin, the Cameroons, French Guinea, the Sierra Leone, Liberia and on the Ivory Coast.

Early travelers observed two uses. Natives made girdle cakes with pulverized dried fruit mixed with salted butter. They also made an infusion. They roasted and pulverized the beans and tossed the powder in boiling water.

A CULTIVATED COMMODITY

The introduction of coffee into Yemen for cultivation probably came during the Abyssinian invasions in the 13th and 14th Centuries. It may have occurred earlier. All is conjecture. The most

Arbre du Café dessiné en Arabie sur le Naturel

solidly established tradition credits Ben Omar al Shadhili as Arabian patron of coffee tree cultivation and coffee drinking.

Yemenites until the 15th Century used only the dried skins of the fruit for infusions, reserving beans for lucrative export to Syria, Persia, Turkey and Europe.

BOTANICAL BURGLINGS

Because of its desirability as a stimulant for more than ten centuries, coffee figured prominently in botanical burglings. The resulting involuntary travels took coffee far afield and promoted its role as one of the plants that changed the world. Transplantation by man spread it around the earth in a band from the Tropic of Capricorn to the Tropic of Cancer.

COFFEE'S GARDEN OF EDEN

Since all the plants for all the coffee in the world started in inner Ethiopia, you would think a recognizable parent plant would still be there. Instead, there are scores of primitive offshoots according to Hugh Rouk, agronomist. "There are so many different ones you can hardly guess which are the original parents. Jungle coffee is high bush, low bush, everything — all as wild as the leopards!"

Until recently Ethiopians took little advantage of their Garden of Eden coffee. They picked a hundred varieties from perhaps 30 species, jumbled them all together. So, 20 years ago, Rouk began teaching students of agriculture to sort out the different beans. He hoped to produce new, exquisite flavors, to give refined American plants a boost from a hardy ancestor.

COFFEE SPECIES

Quality coffee is chiefly the product of *Coffea arabica*. This species, longest known to commerce, has supplied the bulk of world output. It is now cultivated in Kenya, Tanzania, Uganda, Brazil, Colombia, Costa Rica and other tropical and subtropical areas. An interesting, but unsuccessful attempt was even made to grow it in the fields of Dijon!

Two other commercial species should be noted — *robusta* and *liberica*. In quality and subtlety of flavor they are no match for *arabica*. There are, in addition, varieties within these species with characteristics that change with cultural conditions and climate. Of the two, *liberica* has little commercial value.

Robusta is native to Uganda. For centuries the trees have grown on lower altitudes along the shores of Lake Victoria. *Robustas* are increasing in popularity. They are cheaper to grow than *arabicas* and better resist disease and insects. Their quality is good enough to attract more and more consumers in France, Belgium, Holland and Portugal. Other commercially known African *robustas* have also made strides in the world market.

GIANT DWARF?

Another notable species is *caturra*. This 4-foot superproducer from Brazil yields five to seven times more than traditional varieties. It needs no shade. It reaches fruit bearing in three years. It does need better soil, more careful pruning and more regular application of fertilizers and insecticides than other varieties. These conditions make it less desirable in Brazil where plantations are vast and workers cannot baby individual trees. But growers have been introducing *caturra* in Colombia where small landholders can give the care the plants need. *Caturra* now flourishes in Colombia's golden triangle and accounts for almost 30 percent of Colombia's production — second in the world.

CULTURAL CHARACTERISTICS

About a dozen species of coffee are cultivated. In the wild they can grow to 60 feet though 30 feet is usual. Growers prune them to 6-10 feet to ease harvesting by hand. Coffee grows best in sandy, rich, well-drained soil. It thrives in hot, moist places where temperatures do not fall below 55 degrees or go much above 80 and where annual rainfall is 40-70 inches and evenly distributed. It grows especially well on volcanic soil. Frost is a deadly enemy.

Soil, location, and altitude affect cultivation and cup quality. Coffee grown on low swampy coastal lands is generally inferior to that produced at higher altitudes. The finest coffees come from plantations situated three to five thousand and more feet above sea level.

TAB XCV II

Feues de Café

LIFE OF A COFFEE TREE

A plantation tree lives from 25-40 years. Trees are at their best when 10-15 years old. Some growers replace trees after that to strengthen their stock.

Trees bear a few cherries in the third year but are not exploitable until five years from planting. A tree may produce 1-3 pounds a year. Figures vary. Theoretically, a great tree yields 4 or 5 pounds of clean, dry coffee a year. Coffee trees have been known to bear fruit when over 100 years old.

PLANTING COFFEE

Planters grow coffee from seed. Planting can take place almost any time of the year. Trees spend the first year in a nursery. Growth is slow. Seedlings look like bean sprouts three months from sowing and are called "little soldiers." When seedlings are about 15 inches tall, they move to plantations with about 680 trees to the acre. Because they originated as undergrowth trees, planters protect young coffee trees from high winds and hot sun. They plant shade trees in their orchards to make sun hats and windbreaks.

In Colombia, guama trees of the mimosa family with their lacy, parasol-like branches filter the sun and keep the earth moist beneath. In Costa Rica, they plant lemon and orange trees for both food and shade. Elsewhere farmers plant banana trees for shade and food and use the banana leaves to wrap seedlings for transplanting. As shade trees grow older they are pruned to let the sun in.

A HANDSOME SIGHT

Trunks of the coffee tree are short, branches low and falling. The tree is evergreen and has waxen leaves like those of the lemon and laurel. Their upper sides are sparkling and smooth. Flowers are white, fleeting and delicately scented. They appear in dense clusters in flushes three or four times a year. Blooms rarely last more than a day. At the base of fallen flowers the dark green berries develop. When the berries turn red in about six months, the tree looks like a holly.

The soft, sweet glutinous pulp of the berries surrounds two grains lying face to face like halves of peanuts. These are enclosed in a gelatinlike membrane which is removed along with a tough parchmentlike skin and a thin silvery skin before coffee beans are shipped. When only one seed is in the cherry, it is called a peaberry. It is set aside as it brings a higher price.

FRUITING SEASON

Under good conditions, fruiting lasts eight to nine months. Branches show flowers, green fruit and ripe cherries simultaneously. Harvesting lasts five or six months. All producing countries have a major crop season. Where rainfall is limited and seasonal, heaviest harvest occurs then.

HARVESTING BY HAND

Harvesters hand-pick only the ripe cherries, leaving green fruit to ripen. Berries must be picked at their peak for best flavor. Picked too soon, flavor is undeveloped. Picked too late, flavor is bitter. No machine has been invented to do the job.

Nearly 2,000 cherries are needed for a pound of roasted coffee. Good pickers harvest 200 pounds of cherries a day — the equivalent of 40-50 pounds of cleaned coffee. So if you use a pound of coffee each week, you are using the annual crop of about 52 trees each year!

GETTING BEANS READY FOR MARKET

Four processes take place before the coffee cherries are reduced to green beans: removal of the outer skin; fermentation of the gelatinous pulp beneath it; removal of a parchmentlike husk under the pulp; and separation of the bean sections from an inner silver skin. Depulping and hulling take place over a period of days when the beans are spread out to dry. Formerly all was accomplished by hand. Much is now done by machine.

Grading follows for weight and size. Beans are hand inspected to remove off-color or imperfect beans. This is also done by electronic machines that make a preliminary sorting by color and blow out inferior beans they "see." Only beans of proper size, weight and olive green color pass. They are sacked and if they are coming down the mountains in Colombia, the trip is by mule back to the nearest highway, by paddlewheel down a river to the railhead, and by rail to the port where a boat loads them for their destination.

ALL THE COFFEE IN BRAZIL

Coffee lends itself to large scale production. Much is grown on large plantations, some under corporate management. The world's largest plantation in Brazil has more than 4,500,000 trees. Such a large fazenda has its own railway, roads, stores, warehouses and agronomists. During harvests, it hires hundreds of migrant workers.

Not all coffee farms are large, however. A substantial amount of coffee is produced on small family farms in Colombia and Costa Rica.

Carol Nordengren who lived on a coffee farm in Costa Rica describes a typical operation.

"The family I lived with stored green beans in big bags and sold coffee for future delivery the way they sell crops in the United States. They grew their coffee in little plots like apple orchards which they call *coffeetals*. In the middle of the orchard they planted bananas, pulpy oranges and sweet lemons to eat and to shade the coffee trees.

"When harvest time came, they rounded up all the kids and poor people in the neighborhood to pick the ripe berries. Because they picked only ripe berries, they went over the trees again and again. They picked for two weeks straight at a time."

SCIENCE AND POLITICS

For 200 years now growers and scientists have devoted themselves to improving coffee. Brazilians founded the world's first coffee research center. In Colombia a coffee experiment station at Chinchina employs scientists to study all phases of coffee production and processing.

To stabilize prices, coffee producers have entered international agreements. Coffee is a matter for cartels. Coffee is big.

VISIBLE HONORS

Producing countries have memorialized coffee trees on postage stamps. One featured the tree at each stage of growth. Colombian postal officials issued a stamp honoring the tree and 167-year-old Javier Pereira. Sr. Pereira advised would-be imitaters, "Drink coffee and smoke good cigars!"

Statesmen have promoted coffee by posing with coffee trees. Haitian and Kenyan governments have issued currency with pictures of coffee trees. But the most visible honor of all for this fruit product is the vast daily parade of coffee drinkers in 125 countries of the world.

CAFFEINE & CRITICS

Someone has said that bad coffee is an abomination, but good coffee is so glorious that its mere aroma in a sickroom is enough to terrorize death. This is sheer nonsense. It is accurate, however, to say coffee has universal appeal because it is invigorating. An apt derivation for its name is a Turkish word for strength.

A SOBERING INFLUENCE

Until 1669, home beverages included beer and apple and pear ciders. Wherever breakfast brought intoxicants to the table, the introduction of coffee provided a refreshing alternative. An early family receipt book described coffee as a good drink for robust laborers who would despise anything lighter. Coffee was also a valued antidote for contaminated water. It was a matter of folk usage to guard health by making drinks with boiling water.

POTENT POTION

Coffee has had critics. In 1679, the Marseille Medical Faculty declared coffee to be too noxious for the people of Marseille, for their spirits were already too cunning and their blood too hot for them safely to indulge in the drink.

Now and again, princes denounced public coffee houses as seditious places. They believed coffee was powerful enough to arouse the critical temper of malcontents and endanger public tranquility. About the same time, feminine societies, perhaps resenting

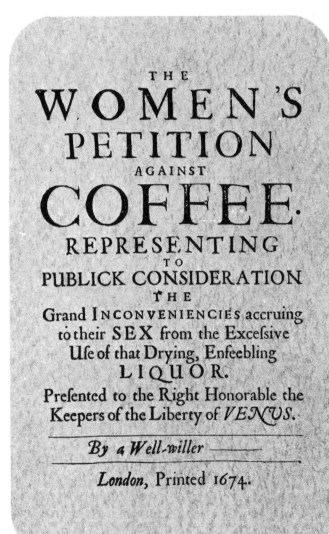

THE
WOMEN'S
PETITION
AGAINST
COFFEE.
REPRESENTING
TO
PUBLICK CONSIDERATION
THE
Grand INCONVENIENCIES accruing to their SEX from the Excesſive Uſe of that Drying, Enfeebling LIQUOR.
Preſented to the Right Honorable the Keepers of the Liberty of VENUS.

By a Well-willer

London, Printed 1674.

the time men spent in coffee houses, damned coffee.
They contended it made men sterile.

HISTORIC BEGINNINGS

Coffee use began in the classical period of
Arabian medicine. Coffee beans had various medical
uses before they made the beverage we drink today.
Rhazes, 9th Century philosopher, astronomer and
superintendent of the Bagdad hospital, mentioned
both the coffee tree and the drink, and physicians
who followed him were aware of them. For a long,
long time, doctors had a proprietary interest in
coffee as a medicine and fought to keep it exclusive.

Herbalists and doctors were among the first users
of coffee in European countries. The French and
English first knew it as a medicine. They believed its
extravagant claims to be a cure for drunkenness,
consumption, catarrh, gout, scurvy and smallpox.
Some believed they should never drink milk with
their coffee for fear of dire consequences like
leprosy. Early in this century there was a curious
story about a French navy doctor who reported that
coffee was a specific for typhoid fever.

ON THE OTHER HAND . . .

In 1835, a florid hymn to coffee appeared in the
Transylvania Journal of Medicine. Translated from the
German, it purported to be an utterance of the son
of Mohammed.

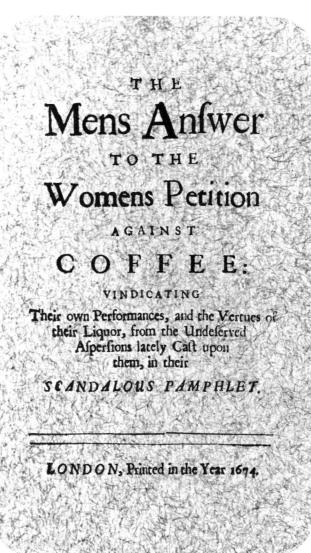

THE
Mens Anſwer
TO THE
Womens Petition
AGAINST
COFFEE:
VINDICATING
Their own Performances, and the Vertues of
their Liquor, from the Undeſerved
Aſperſions lately Caſt upon
them, in their
SCANDALOUS PAMPHLET.

LONDON, Printed in the Year 1674.

Coffee is the beverage of the people of God, and the cordial of his servants who thirst for wisdom. When coffee is infused into the bowl, it exhales the odor of musk, and is of the color of ink. The truth is not known except to the wise, who drink it from the foaming coffee cup. God has deprived fools of coffee, who with invincible obstinacy condemn it as injurious . . In it will we drown our adversities, and in its fire consume our sorrows.

Ridiculous, exclaimed Dr. William Alcott, fiercest coffee fighter of his time. The fact that any one could write a hymn to coffee convinced him that the man was under the influence of a narcotic drink. He damned the whole lot of Turks and Arabs.

MATERIA MEDICA

Coffee properly belonged among the articles of *materia medica,* he said. As proof, he cited physicians, medical dictionaries, the *Journal of Health, Catechism of Health,* French and Italian medical writers and Linnaeus. Besides, he said, he had killed two rabbits with coffee. He neglected to say fatal overdoses of coffee or caffeine had not been reported in humans. He only regretted his experiments had not been more extensive. He vent his special rage on Senex, who wrote anonymously for the Boston *Medical and Surgical Journal.*

Senex had the temerity in this naughty world of excess and intemperance to suggest that although water, pure and drunk at the fountain, was the finest of drinks, a drink had other legitimate uses.

What about condiment and refreshment? he asked. Couldn't every form of exciting drink, even spirits, be useful in moderate quantities? Doesn't a man at times need something besides water to give relish to food, aid digestion, promote appetite and restore the body when he is weary of physical or mental labor?

MENTAL HEALTH ASSET

Many have disagreed with Alcott's conclusion that coffee drinking abridges human happiness and human life. A contemporary doctor and professor of occupational health at a Western university cites pluses for coffee.

Coffee breaks are an important mental health asset, she says. Coffee contains between 100 and 150 milligrams of caffeine in an average cup, an amount at the lower limit of a therapeutic dose. Drinking a strong alkaloid like this every day exerts a pharmacological effect.

According to the professor, results of coffee consumption show up in clearer, more rapid thinking; forestalling of sleep and fatigue; a prolonged intellectual effort; better association of ideas; a sharper appreciation of sensory stimuli, increased motor activity and a diminution of reaction time to stimuli.

INDIVIDUAL REACTIONS TO CAFFEINE

French gastronomist Brillat-Savarin in his famous *Physiology of Taste* described coffee's known power to

excite cerebral activity. Some people, he observed, are too highly stimulated by coffee to tolerate the habit. Others can't function well without their morning cup.

He cited Voltaire and Buffon. To coffee, Voltaire may have owed his admirable clarity; Buffon, the harmony of his literary style. Many of the latter's descriptions of animals in *Essays on Man* were written "in a state of extraordinary cerebral exaltation."

Brillat-Savarin opined that a strong man could drink two bottles of wine a day and still live a long time, but the same amount of coffee would make him imbecilic. As for himself, he could not drink coffee without being overstimulated. He told of preparing himself for a demanding editing job by fortifying himself with two large cups of very strong coffee. He did not sleep again for 40 hours, all the while finding himself in a state of mental excitement.

COFFEE RESEARCH

Periodically news stories give coffee a bad press, last the day and disappear without having established data to prove or disprove sweeping ill effects.

What are the facts? Copious research lights up every corner of the world of coffee from plantations and laboratories to the man on the street.

Studies reveal that people drink coffee, not because their bodies demand it, but for a range of psychological reasons. The daily practice of drinking a hot, aromatic, pleasantly flavored, rich looking beverage in cheerful surroundings establishes a comfortable pattern. It starts the day well. During working hours, it brightens breaks from routine. It is a welcome excuse for lingering over dinner at day's end.

A researcher studying typists, discovered an excess of coffee slowed speed while one or two cups helped typists improve speed and accuracy of performance. Coffee benefits normal people who simply find it pleasant.

PHARMACOLOGICAL THERAPEUTICS

Studies abound on chemical therapeutics called xanthines. The pharmacological bases of these xanthines — caffeine, theophylline and theobromine — are present in many plants widely distributed around the world. Where these plants are native, populations use them in beverages. Some, like coffee, tea and cocoa, are consumed all over the world. All three contain caffeine. Tea contains theophylline also and a six-ounce cup of tea has about 90 mg. caffeine. Cocoa contains theobromine.

Other caffeine beverages include maté, a national drink in South America. In the Sudan, natives chew and swallow the extract from kola nuts which contain about two percent caffeine.

In the Amazon basin, the *Paullinia sorbilis,* used for a beverage, has a large amount of caffeine. Many soft drinks are appealing simply because they contain from 30-50 mg. caffeine in a six-ounce glass.

IMPRESSIVE MEDICAL RESEARCH

The bibliography of medical research papers in scholarly publications is thorough and impressive.

Research points to effects of caffeine on the central nervous system, the cardiovascular system, smooth muscles, voluntary muscles, diuretic action, gastric secretion, blood clotting, metabolism, tolerance and toxicology. In sum, the pharmacological actions of the xanthines find many applications.

SOME CONCLUSIONS DRAWN FROM STUDIES

The most popular xanthine beverages are coffee, tea and cocoa. While most people drink coffee for its stimulation, they may be unaware of this effect. The degree of stimulation varies from person to person, depending on temperament. Some suffer insomnia; some do not. For some the stimulation precludes adequate relaxation.

Children are more susceptible than grownups. Normally they are excitable without stimulation.

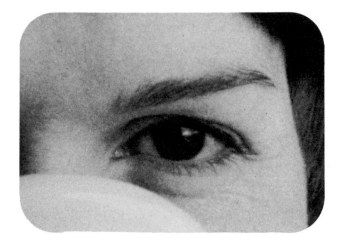

Also, drinking xanthine beverages interferes with their eating foods necessary to their development. They should not drink coffee, tea or cocoa.

It is commonly understood that persons with active peptic ulcers should not drink caffeine beverages. Even decaffeinated coffees are suspect because of constituents other than xanthines present in them.

The most cogent finding is this: **there is no evidence that drinking coffee is in itself any way harmful.**

The feeling of well being and the increased performance which it affords, although possibly obtained at the expense of decreased efficiency later in the day, are experiences few people would care to abandon. Most authorities take the attitude that absolute denial of coffee to persons who enjoy it may be more disturbing than any stimulant in the drink.

A VERITABLE WHODUNNIT

Sophisticated research reveals that coffee is but one among many factors among a whole array of conditions. Several years ago there was a mild storm in the press about a possible link between coffee drinking and heart problems. Using a computer to check records of 250,000 patients, Kaiser Health Foundation doctors could find no link. They concluded it seemed premature to add to privations already inflicted on actual or potential coronary disease victims by denying them the solace of their morning coffee.

A leading American heart specialist also doubts that coffee causes heart attacks. The culprit, he says, is the nervous, high-strung personality of the coffee drinker.

GOOD HABITS COUNT

Dr. J. G. Molner, medical columnist, once responded to a reader that coffee is a good pick-me-up because it mildly stimulates the heart and circulation and wakes up the brain.

Tolerances vary. Some of us can drink quite a lot; others can't. A tense, high-strung person may have difficulty getting to sleep after drinking coffee. Others have no trouble.

It is rather common in medical practice to talk to people who complain of being perpetually nervous and find that they drink a great deal of tea or coffee. They are being overstimulated.

For such people he recommended cutting down or not drinking coffee, tea and cola drinks. For those

who benefit from stimulation, he suggested two or three cups but less than five during the day. Everything depends on whether you want to increase or decrease stimulation.

IT DEPENDS ON YOU

Coffee, in short, is neither healthy nor unhealthy. Everything depends on the amount, the circumstances, and your makeup. You have to be guided by your own individual reaction to the drink.

An important thing to remember is that caffeine is not exclusive to coffee but is in tea, cocoa and cola drinks, as well as in some common medicines. One common cold remedy tablet, for example, contains about a half grain (32 milligrams) of caffeine. On prescription, you could ingest 4½ grains (288 milligrams) during a 24-hour period. If you are caffeine sensitive, you need to keep this in mind.

UNCONSCIOUS EXCESS

In a talk before the American Psychiatric Association, a Walter Reed Army Hospital psychiatrist cited the case of an army officer. He had taken calm-down drugs for 14 months without effect. His dizziness, butterflies in the stomach, diarrhea and other complaints disappeared when he stopped drinking about 14 cups of coffee and three or four cola drinks each day. He had been consuming 1200 milligrams of caffeine daily. Excess was his problem, not coffee or cola.

An interesting fact is this: if you drink three cups of coffee, have a cola drink and take two over-the-counter headache tablets in one morning, your intake of caffeine approximates 500 mg. Many Americans exceed that. Few realize that cold and headache tablets contain caffeine.

ONE FOR THE ROAD?

One can also ask, "Does a cup of coffee ever sober up a drunk? Is coffee the best for the road?"

Quite simply, no. Dr. Ronald Laing, medical director of industrial programs of the Addiction Research Foundation in North Bay, Ontario, reports:

The result is that instead of having a sleepy drunk you have a wide awake drunk. We tend to laugh at such a situation. Actually, it is serious. This person should be sleeping off his sedation, but is now awake and thinks he can drive if you can just help him to the car and get the key in the right place.

Rutgers Center of Alcohol Studies concurred. Alcohol enters the bloodstream fast but the body takes time to get rid of it. No black coffee will hasten the process.

WHAT ABOUT DECAFFEINATION?

Does decaffeination solve all problems? Popularity of decaffeinated coffee has increased

steadily since first patents were granted in 1908. Today decaffeinated coffee accounts for 18 percent of the total cups consumed in the home where three-fourths of all coffee is consumed.

DECAFFEINATION PROCESS

Green beans are softened and heated under steam pressure for five hours to 21 percent moisture. They are then wetted with water, perhaps treated with ammonia or acids and a caffeine solvent such as alcohol, trichlorethylene (TCE), chloroform, or benzene. This solvent is steam evaporated and distilled from the beans and the caffeine collected. The decaffeinated beans are then dried, roasted and ground like other beans.

The process is expensive. Experts say it's as difficult to extract the last 2 percent of the caffeine as to extract the first 95-97 percent.

A DIFFERENT TASTE

According to John Adinolfi, chemist for a coffee association, decaffeinated coffee tastes slightly different than other coffee because decaffeination removes some of the oils and waxes found in coffee beans. This affects roasting.

Health-oriented researchers point out that traces of trichlorethylene allowed by government rules to remain in the beans are ingested in decaffeinated coffee. Coffee connoisseurs say they can taste the solvent

and look down their noses at the fact that processors often use *robusta*, not *arabica*, beans.

IS THERE A GOOD WORD?

"Can you say something good about decaffeinated coffee?" we asked a coffee specialty shop owner.

"Yes," he replied and explained two current methods. "American processors use caffeine-removing solvents. The Swiss have a secret method which is not patented. It removes 97 percent of the caffeine and, I think, is a better process. If you have our decaffeinated coffee in the morning, you'll go right back to sleep. Melitta sells it, we sell it and so do other specialty houses. We ship Colombian beans to Switzerland. They process them and ship them back. About half the cost is in the transportation."

We tried his decaffeinated coffee. It was smooth and pleasant as he promised, but its taste disappeared the moment we swallowed it.

PERSISTENT QUESTIONS

Even decaffeinated coffee irritates some people. How many is unknown. Medical researchers working on the problem so far have discovered that an "unknown ingredient in coffee appears to cause as much stomach acid secretion as caffeine."

The best advice is still: know yourself and understand that drinking coffee is an individual matter.

SUBSTITUTES & STRETCHERS

Wars and bad times always disrupt coffee consumption. Transportation becomes difficult or impossible and the search is on for substitutes and stretchers. Some substitutes merely extend coffee and reduce cost. Some have been preferred to coffee. In the past, some of the best came from dried pulp and parchment of coffee cherries.

PRICE AND PROCLAMATION PROBLEMS

In pioneer America, the cost of transportation by pack horse made coffee prohibitive and substitutes desirable. Another deterrent came in 1837 with the Edict of New Lebanon, forbidding coffee to all Shakers save those over 60. Elders weren't expected to break the habit of a lifetime. Promulgators of the edict wanted to stress reliance on God, not coffee, for strength and inspiration. So, Shakers substituted corn, rye, other grains, peas, chicory root and seeds of locust trees and goosegrass.

DRINK WATER!

About the same time, a Boston cookbook was recommending economical substitutes:

. . . some use dry brown bread crusts and roast them; others soak rye grain in rum and roast it; others roast peas in the same way as coffee. None of these are very good and peas so used are considered unhealthy. Where there is a large family of apprentices and workmen, and coffee is very dear, it may be worthwhile to use substitutes, or to mix them half and half with coffee; but, after all, the best economy is to go without.

Another vintage cook agreed that "the best substitute is toasted crust of bread, but it is cheaper to drink water."

EUROPEAN SUBSTITUTES

In Europe, coffee substitutes were almost as old as coffee. When Germans could not get coffee, they made beverages with barley, wheat, corn, chicory and dried figs.

Substitutes appeared in England after the great London fire. In 1719, these included betony root; sassafras and sugar; and bocket, a hot drink infused with powdered orchis or sassafras and served with milk and sugar.

HANDY SUBSTITUTES

Dried roots of "teeth of the lion," your common dooryard dandelion, have substituted for coffee. So, if you have these beautiful weeds on your lawn, dig the roots up, clean and bake them brown and grind them. You can mix them with coffee as you would chicory.

You can also roast and grind carrots, parsnips, beets and mangel-wurzel; beans, lupin and other leguminous seeds; cereal grains; seeds of broom, fenugreek and iris; acorns and soybeans.

Germans value acorn coffee as wholesome and nourishing. They shell the acorns, slowly dry them and roast them in a closed vessel. They grind the roasted nuts like coffee, sometimes add them to coffee and sweeten with sugar. Processors once ran afoul of the national fodder department because acorns were also valued animal food.

At one time manufacturers made pellets to simulate coffee beans. They ground peas, pea hulls, cereals, bran and cereal wastes and compacted them with molasses and other sticky stuff. One inventor made pellets by mixing chicory with wheat flour, ground beans and a little coffee. Some pellets looked exactly like coffee beans right down to the bean crease.

ADULTERANTS

The fact that coffee is ground invites adulterants. Mixing ground coffee with adulterants made more than one man rich on sawdust, grindings of prepared carrots, peas, acorns, malted grains, mill sweepings, flour and vegetable hulls. A popular product contained roasted peas, rye, chicory, "other ingredients" not named, and a little roasted coffee. One adulterant, a mixture of dry orris root and roasted rye, did have good flavor. The Javanese used roasted seeds of a leguminous tree with good results. An expensive adulterant contained dried ox blood and horse liver.

HEALTH AND ERSATZ COFFEES

"Health" coffees have used, besides seeds, nuts and chicory root: date pits, potatoes, turnips, almonds and figs. When hawthorn berries were favored, officials in Germany designated them as important resources to be protected by the police.

In 1917, a German firm complained that competitors were adding too much heather to ersatz coffee! The use of such unusual materials caused the *Committee for Coffee, Tea and Other Ersatz Materials* to forbid the use of sawdust, peat, grape skins, leached tanbark, henbane, shells of hazelnuts and walnuts, and pits of cherries and plums.

A PERFECT COMPANION

The best substitute and additive is chicory. Many in France, Southern Germany, Belgium, Holland, Switzerland and Great Britain prefer their coffee mixed with it. For them, chicory improves; it does not adulterate. It has stood the test of time and has the approval of medical researchers, public health doctors and pharmacologists. Gourmets recommend it. M.F.K. Fisher believes any coffee made with chicory is better than perfect.

CICHORIUM INTYBUS

What is chicory? A perennial plant, *Cichorium intybus* has thick roots and grows in quantity in

Michigan and in Europe. Its common names are succory, coffeeweed and blue sailor. It is related to that roadside flower of heavenly blue that makes you wish the passage were less swift for you to see it the more.

Chicory has been in larders and gardens for centuries, cultivated for both roots and leaves. A 4000-year-old papyrus mentions chicory. Now in Leipzig, the document extols its wholesomeness and use as a remedy. For the Egyptians, it was an emblem of fidelity.

Aristophanes made note of chicory as did Horace. Roman soldiers carried chicory among their rations. Chicory grew in Charlemagne's herb garden and in the gardens of Louis XIV.

At the end of the 17th Century, the Dutch gave chicory its first industrial treatment and Napoleon later encouraged the trend.

NAPOLEONIC COFFEE

In the early 19th Century, chicory came into common use when Napoleon's Continental System deprived Frenchmen of pure coffee. As a result, coffee was mixed with equal parts of chicory.

Grocers and cooks embraced chicory with a passion. They swore that coffee mixed with chicory not only tasted better but was better for health. European bakers used powdered chicory to flavor dark rye breads, cookies and cakes; and cooks, to season soups, meats and vegetables. When the Continental System fell, French cooks continued to use chicory, mixing it with ground coffee. To circumvent this practice, their employers bought coffee beans, but cooks found mills especially made for chicory and went on adding it to coffee.

HARVESTING AND PROCESSING

Chicory is harvested much like sugar beets. Its raw roots are sliced, kiln dried, roasted and ground like coffee beans. Ten pounds of roots produce two pounds of chicory.

As a filler, chicory stretches coffee and adds body and aroma. Alone, it is a substitute for coffee and has itself been adulterated with rye, wheat and beans and been colored with iron-bearing earths, burned sugar and Venetian red.

CHICORY'S CHARACTER

"Is chicory bitter?" many ask. Not at all. It has a good caramel taste and leaves a half sweet, pleasantly smooth aftertaste. It has some food value and gives coffee a richer color, bite and body. Adding it to coffee is a good way to reduce caffeine if you tend to drink too much full strength coffee. Added to dark roast, it tends to cut the char or bitterness.

Opposition to chicory results largely from blindspots and prejudice. We have heard some retailers explain the absence of chicory in their shops by dredging up stigmas connected with Civil War economy and concluding, "It's a weed. We don't like the taste."

SOME MEDICAL RESEARCHERS SAY . . .

Chicory is a natural ally of the body, having numerous beneficial effects, according to formal studies made by doctors in France, Italy and Germany.

Classed as a medical depurative, chicory contains a purifying agent called *inulin*. Added to coffee, it tones down coffee acids in the stomach. Chicory also exerts an anti-fermentative function and acts as an equilibrator during the last phase of digestion. It is tonic to the liver and favors bile secretion. It stimulates digestive functions and intensifies salivation. It has cleansing virtues and effects a soothing action on the nervous system. It is an inner detoxicator.

Chicory separates milk and fat into small flakes, guaranteeing digestibility. It helps dissolve fats in butter. Its presence in coffee helps drinkers assimilate milk.

Medically, there are no counter indications.

TASTE TESTING

You can find coffee roasters who will blend chicory with coffee to your taste. Because we wanted to make our own blend, we began by blending small amounts of ground chicory with whatever coffee beans we were grinding.

A coffee retailer with excellent credentials suggested that the best way to find out how much chicory to add is to start with one tablespoon of chicory to every five of ground coffee and keep on increasing the proportions until results are pleasing. An English cookbook suggests beginning with two ounces of chicory to each pound of coffee.

An excellent French product is 60 percent coffee and 40 percent chicory. A Swiss version has 65 percent coffee and 35 percent chicory. In the United States, proportions vary by regions. In the North, preference is for 85 percent coffee and 15 percent chicory; in the Mid-Atlantic, it is 75/25; in the South, 55/45. Price lists for chicory in 1975 were about half what they were for good coffee by the pound.

EXPERIMENTING WITH CHICORY

Chicory yields lavishly when infused in either hot or cold water. A kilo of dried chicory is 70 percent soluble matter that melts when brewed. A pure brew is heavy and dark which augurs well for a rich, attractive looking drink. Because chicory improves flavor, experimenting is in order.

We use the cold water method to prepare coffee essence. At first we filtered ground coffee simultaneously with ground chicory, increasing proportions of chicory until we had half coffee and half chicory. Then we reduced the amount of chicory to taste. In the process, we discovered that chicory's thick, chocolaty liquid clogged the felt filter. To prevent this, we soaked chicory separately in cold water for a half hour, recovered the essence through a fine sieve and added it to prepared coffee essence in a carafe. Then, all we have to do is pour a measured amount of coffee-chicory essence into a cup and add boiling water to make an excellent cup of coffee.

COMMERCIAL COFFEE SUBSTITUTES

Coffee substitutes on the market are vaunted as health foods and "family drinks for all ages." We have tried them without enthusiasm. The caffeine-free Postum we knew as children is available, its ingredients unchanged. It now boasts vitamins.

Postum was the brain child of Charles Post, farm machinery salesman. In 1893, he mixed his famous three — bran, wheat and molasses — as a nutritional substitute for coffee and called it Postum. Along with two early breakfast cereals, it was the basis for the fortune which his daughter, Marjorie Merriweather Post, built into General Foods Corp. Postum had a remarkable influence on her financial health whether she drank it or not.

A German product, labeled "instant cereal beverage," is made from roasted and ground malted barley, barley, chicory, rye and molasses and has no stimulants. It is expensive and tends to cake. Taken without milk or sugar, it is sharp and heavy.

Recent instant coffee introductions by major coffee companies have ingredient listings that sound like chemists' dreams and include chocolate, cocoanut, orange and other flavorings. They have romantic names.

WHATEVER HAPPENED TO . . . ?

The ultimate substitute was suggested in a 1959 headline in an American newspaper: 5-CENT CUP OF COFFEE DUE SOON. The UPI story from Washington reported:

The 5-cent cup of coffee may not be a thing of the past after all. Government researchers say a synthetic coffee made from wheat and barley and costing much less than the real stuff could be only months away!

Heaven forbid!

BROWNED, BLENDED & BREWED

You are going to have fun exploring this whole business of "Browned, Blended and Brewed" because it is the only way to find the coffee you like best.

Start at the beginning. Go back to the bean and confront it in specialty coffee stores. Find out how many kinds there are, where they come from around the world. Explore the ways beans are roasted and what roast goes with what distinguishable taste. Learn what individual grinds do for coffee and how they influence your coffee maker.

In the exploration, you will discover a delightful fact: by sampling many kinds of beans, different roasts and ways of making coffee, you will find not just one coffee you like best but a number of them. Your favorite drink, you know, is not a single instrument but a whole orchestra.

SEARCH FOR GREAT COFFEES

Our own curiosity about coffee started with comparisons of various canned coffees in supermarkets. We tried one brand after another. Few cans described the origin of the coffee inside. We found ourselves making buying decisions on catchy advertising, attractive packaging, discount couponing and sales. We really didn't know what we were drinking.

We read coffee critics in the press who charged that canned coffee was the mass merchandiser's loss leader designed to attract store patronage; that it was a blend of underroasted, inferior beans; that it

actually tasted of the nitrogen packers use to forestall staling in vacuum cans. In short, they said, customers were buying a pig in a poke.

We didn't think canned coffee was all that bad. We knew it didn't always measure up to coffee served in fine restaurants or in espresso bars.

What, then, was the difference in taste between canned coffees and coffee beans? Was it so fabulous? Could anybody taste the difference? Our search began with only taste and sensitivity for our guides.

WHAT WE ALL BRING TO COFFEE TASTING

Tests show no two people have exactly the same threshhold for taste and aroma. Nor does their sensitivity to taste remain constant. Palates change three times a day. This may be why we prefer stronger coffee for breakfast.

Taste buds are small, very sensitive to temperature, and easily overcome by flavor. If we burn our mouths, our taste buds fail for a day or two. The back of the tongue registers bitterness or freshness of flavors. The tip signals sweetness. Sides pick up staleness and sourness. We taste the sweet before the bitter, but the bitter lasts longer.

We use the back of our mouths and nasal passages in classifying aroma. The sense of taste fades as we age, and we use more sugar in coffee to compensate. Youngsters more quickly identify sugar solutions than the elderly.

In short, many elements affect taste evaluation: differences in metabolism, health, hunger, fatigue, age, sex, and previous ingestion of stimulating sweets, sours, salts, nicotine and alcohol. Personal attitudes, prejudices, cultural standards, customs, susceptibility to advertising and labeling, openness to new taste experiences, influences of environmental and service factors — all play a part, too.

That is why the search for a great cup of coffee involves you very personally. You have your own key. That is why the best coffee for you is the coffee you like best.

BEWILDERING ARRAY AT SPECIALTY STORES

We began our search at coffee specialty stores. A whole new world of taste possibilities opened — bins of roasted beans with as many as 30 countries

represented; a wealth of fragrances, to say nothing of whole arrays of paraphernalia for storing, grinding, brewing and serving coffee.

Tantalizing aroma led us into stores that operated old fashioned coffee roasters in full view. We heard coffee beans jingling around like so many small rocks in a cement mixer, popping and cracking as they turned and roasted. We knew we had come in the nick of time.

"The coffee merchant who doesn't have his own roaster", observed a wiseacre, "is like a restaurateur without a stove. He has to roast and do it often to have fresh beans." Failing that, he must have a supplier who roasts often and delivers swiftly.

We saw coffees labeled with country of origin. Some stores added grade and size information and presented jargon for us to decode — Colombia Excelso, India Peaberry, Colombia Maragogipe, and such.

COFFEE TALK

Many coffee houses have catalogs or price listings and descriptions of varieties they sell. The word *acidity* occurs often. What does it mean?

"When we use the word *acidity,* we're talking about good cup quality," said an expert. "I would use the word *sharpness* instead. When I talk about acidity, I'm not talking about coffee that hits the back of your tongue like sandpaper. I'm talking about coffee that has a clean, sharp, pleasing, not bitter, taste."

High grown coffees have more natural acidity than low grown varieties. Brazilian coffees have much less acidity, and robustas have the least. A light roast is more acid than a dark roast. Carrots and coffee have comparable acidity, but the appeal of coffee is more complex. It relies on color, heat and aroma as well as flavor.

AROMA

"Chemists have described coffee aroma as a bouquet with hundreds of organic flavor notes measured in a few parts per million — all highly perishable," our coffeeman continued. "The absence of a single note or presence of a foreign note warns that all is not right. These chemical aromas can be recognized from coffee to coffee."

Don't let all this complexity alarm you. You don't have to be a chemist or have special ability to be quite discriminating.

QUALITY VARIABLES

How do you get top quality coffee? Every time you buy coffee beans in a specialty store, ask the clerk for information about them. Here are some things to keep in mind.

1. Origin. There are too many variables for you to judge quality by country of origin alone. Coffee from the Antigua region of Guatemala is favored by one retailer. Another says Arabian coffee is best. Colombia has good coffee, too. But coffee crops like everything that grows vary from year to year in the best of regions. Coffee even varies from roast to roast.

2. High and Low Grown. High grown coffee has more consistent quality. It is more acid, more flavorsome and aromatic. Beans are small, hard, firm and dense. Low grown coffees have larger, lighter, softer beans, are apt to taste bland and swampy and are less expensive. You can actually see the differences.

TRUST THE SELLER

If you don't know beans, know the man who sells them. Specialty shops generally buy top grades. In the final analysis, you have to rely on the expertise, integrity and good taste of the man who sells the beans. The good coffeeman takes years to develop a reputation for handling quality coffees. He doesn't add cheap fillers to high grade beans. He doesn't tell you, you can store roasted beans for months without losing flavor.

VARIETIES

There are two major varieties — *arabica* and *robusta*. The patrician arabicas that grow at high altitudes and fetch higher prices comprise the main stock in specialty stores.

Commercial firms use the robustas mainly for instant coffee. They are more bitter, have twice the caffeine content of arabicas and are lower in price. The better robustas are bland, neutral or strawlike in flavor.

THE WHOLE EXPERIENCE?

If you want to have the whole experience from green beans to cup, buy green beans at specialty stores that do their own roasting. Look for beans with a waxy appearance. This means they will roast well.

Some green beans can be stored for years and will improve and mellow with age like wine. It is said that Java's most famous aged beans were 12 years old. Old beans are small and shriveled. Technicians say they are "well knitted."

If you want to roast your own, use a frying pan roaster with a hand crank. It takes only 16 minutes at the right temperature. We have found no good motor driven mini-roasters on the market. You can, of course, roast beans in your oven, but this is very unsatisfactory since beans must be kept moving to roast evenly.

SELECTING COFFEE BEANS

Only by buying and tasting many different coffees will you come to know their character. Some coffees have strength. Some have flavor. Others have distinc- tive aroma and taste. There are as many variations in taste and appearance as there are variations in wines. Here's a *Coffee Buyer's Guide* for a starter.

COFFEE BUYER'S GUIDE

Specialty stores offer many varieties. These include milds and neutrals, many of which are listed here with their distinctive features as described by expert buyers and tasters.

MILDS:	In general, *milds* are arabicas and often represent the highest quality coffee in a blend. They have fine flavor, aroma and abundant life. Many have more strength, body, aroma and acidity than the *neutrals*.

ORIGIN	DISTINCTIVE FEATURES	YOUR RATING
AMERICAS	**Mexico** High grown beans: mild, mellow with full, rich body; pleasant sharpness, good aroma. Compare with best in the world. Superior Mexican coffees come from: *Pluma, Oaxaca:* small, fancy beans, sharply acid, good blenders; pleasant nutlike flavor *Jalapa:* heavy, rich flavor *Uruapan:* exquisite bouquet	
CENTRAL AMERICA	**Guatemala** High grown; mild or mellow flavor and aroma; full, heavy body. Beans make beautiful roast and excellent cup. Some believe it to be best coffee in the world. *Antigua:* small, hard beans; spicy, sharp, acid; excellent aroma and flavor *Coban:* handsome large roast; heavy body; mellow flavor *All Areas:* Maragogipe — a giant bean variety; medium in body, aroma and flavor; often advertised as sweet and smooth	

ORIGIN	DISTINCTIVE FEATURES	YOUR RATING
CENTRAL AMERICA (*continued*)	***Nicaragua*** Premium beans are large, fancy roasters, boldly acid, full bodied and fragrant. Similar to Guatemalan Antigua yet distinctive in taste. A large portion is exported to Holland, Italy and Finland.	
	El Salvador Finest high grown beans are full bodied, aromatic; have smooth, neutral flavor, somewhat sweet. Good blender and filler *Santiago de Maria:* washed beans are stylish; excellent quality	
	Costa Rica Famous for high quality, desirable beans with beautiful, often pungent aroma. Full bodied, mild flavored, sharply tart cup whose taste does not linger. Beans add strength when blended with milder coffees. One expert rates Costa Rican coffee with Sumatran and Mocha as the three most aromatic.	
SOUTH AMERICA	***Colombia*** High grown, fancy grade beans rank with finest in the world. They produce one-fourth more liquor of a given strength than Brazilian Santos with much finer flavor and delightful fragrance. Taste is considered "middle ground" or standard among arabicas. Other arabicas are milder or sharper. Best beans come from Medellin, Armenia and Manizales. *Supremo* has large, flat uniform beans, somewhat rare, light in body, smooth, rich, aromatic. *Extra* has flat, medium size beans with or without medium or Caracol beans.	

ORIGIN	DISTINCTIVE FEATURES	YOUR RATING
SOUTH AMERICA *(continued)*	**Colombia** *(continued)* *Excelso* has large and medium mixture of Supremo and Extra beans with or without Caracol. Excelso represents 80% of the exports to the United States. *Maragogipe* is biggest of all Colombian beans; said to rival finest Javas.	
	Peru Best comes from Chauchamayo. Beans range from medium to bold in size. One expert describes it as mild and heavy with a naturally sweet taste, "but doesn't hang on like Kenyan."	
	Venezuela Generally a good, mild coffee next to Brazilian Santos in quality and price. Blue beans from Caracas have a highly regarded light, acidy flavor. Beans from Merida have a delicate flavor and high acidity prized by connoisseurs as among the world's best. Limited quantities are aged for years for the gourmet trade that seeks heavy flavor.	
WEST INDIES	**Dominican Republic** Large beans have good body, strong flavor; used extensively in French roasts.	
	Guadeloupe In France you can buy these glossy, hard, elephant size beans. They are dazzling and have an outstanding aroma. First class Bonifieur beans have excellent quality; rarely seen in United States.	
	Haiti Beans make good looking roast with rich, medium acid, slightly sweet flavor; used extensively in French roasts. Best comes from Gonave.	

ORIGIN	DISTINCTIVE FEATURES	YOUR RATING
WEST INDIES *(continued)*	***Jamaica*** Blue Mountain beans, grown on a single hillside under ideal conditions, produce a fancy roast with more flavor oils than most other beans. Taste is full, mellow, rich without bitterness. Some say this rare coffee is coveted by connoisseurs the world over not because of its sheer flavor but because there's not enough to go around. In 1973, the Japanese had an ongoing bid, 25 cents a pound above the highest offers. Limited quantities are available in the United States. Very expensive. Be suspicious. It's hard to get.	
	Puerto Rico Large bean makes a fancy roast with heavy body, unique flavor; rather smoother than beans from Caracas.	
PACIFIC REGION	***Hawaii – Kona*** Highly fertilized lava soil produces large beans that make handsome roasts with mildly sharp, medium body and striking winy smooth flavor.	
AFRICA	***Angola*** Angola produces robustas that are medium size and produce a heavy flavored cup. Angola was the world's fourth largest exporter of coffee until civil uprising in 1975 when shipments ceased.	
	Congo Coffee is similar to Kenyan — bold, good looking arabica beans, producing more acidity in the cup than Mexican or Colombian coffees and having a sharp flavor. Robusta coffees constitute major crop. These are used in processing instant coffee.	

ORIGIN	DISTINCTIVE FEATURES	YOUR RATING
AFRICA *(continued)* 	***Ethiopia*** Mocha Harar, the original mocha, has a distinctive, heavy body, pungent, winy flavor and rich aroma. It is similar to Arabian Mocha but sharper, with delicious flavor. Three grades: *extra sifted*, all large beans; *short berry Harar*, all small beans; and *longberry Harar*, medium size beans.	
	Kenya Small to medium beans from mountain range that includes Mt. Kilimanjaro. Make a rich, full bodied, slightly sweet, aromatic cup with pleasantly tart maple sugary, vanilla-like overtones. Smooth lingering after-taste. So distinctively sharp that you either like it or hate it. Blends well with medium and mild bodied coffees. Kenyan coffee has real character in its high grown coffees. An expert will show you a sample and point out fine striations on the bean. "These are called character lines," he will tell you.	
	Tanzania Peaberries make a handsome roast. This is the most aromatic coffee we have had — from minute it is ground right through brewing. Strong, but smooth taste; more acidy than most. Fairly expensive. Useful to beef up milder coffees or commercial blends.	
NEAR EAST 	***Yemen*** Mocha beans — small and irregular in size — produce a rough roast with quakers. Roasters expect to find a few sticks and some dirt in every sack. Otherwise, they wonder whether they have the real thing. But beans are stylish and produce a distinctive, creamy rich, chocolaty,	

ORIGIN	DISTINCTIVE FEATURES	YOUR RATING
NEAR EAST (continued)	**Yemen** bittersweet, smooth flavor. Very aromatic with heavy body and unique acid accent that adds desired sharpness and aroma to any blend. *Mocha Java* Mocha alone has a little too much acid for some but combines very well with Java which is not quite acid enough. Together they make one of the world's most popular blends, a connoisseur's favorite. Different roasters roast them separately and then blend the beans in various proportions to achieve a balance of flavor and smoothness. Taste will vary considerably from place to place. By law, blenders must put in more Mocha than Java and mention Mocha first. One expert says the best blend is three parts Mocha to two parts Java. Supply of Mocha beans from Yemen has diminished in the last few years as coffee plantations have been replaced by faster growing, more profitable narcotic Kat. When retailers can't get Mocha from Yemen, they import from other locations like Ethiopia to make up the difference. Ethiopian Mochas are winy and not as good.	
ASIA	*India* Peaberry is an unusual, completely oval bean that makes a good roast. Sharp and harsh, but aromatic in the cup and deep in color.	

ORIGIN	DISTINCTIVE FEATURES	YOUR RATING
ASIA *(continued)*	**India** *(continued)* *Mysore* Beans produce medium bodied, strong flavored liquor.	
	Java Only arabica beans from Java can be called Java, according to USDA. They are small, blue to yellow in color and make a smooth roast. They provide the mild, mellow flavor and pungent aroma in Mocha Java blend. Robusta beans from Java, called Indonesians, are poor in quality and used as fillers.	
	Sumatra Sumatra produces several arabica coffees which some connoisseurs consider the most desirable in the world. Large uniform beans have deep, heavy, syrupy rich flavor reminiscent of milk chocolate and have positive aroma. Retailers feature high quality beans from Mandheling.	
	New Guinea Mild, high grown beans are tasty, medium bodied and have rich flavor and aroma similar to Colombian.	
	Celebes Kalossi is considered among finest of coffees, medium bodied, hearty aroma, full deep flavor. *Boengie* Arabica coffee has same characteristics as Mandheling. Heavy body	

NEUTRALS:

These are Brazilian coffees that give bulk to blends. They are mild flavored, light bodied. Beans, in general, are smaller, more uneven than *milds*.

ORIGIN	DISTINCTIVE FEATURES	YOUR RATING
BRAZIL	*Brazil* Brazilian beans are the commercial blender's base. Few retail specialty houses sell them because coffee graders say they produce a soft, flat, mediocre liquor generally lacking in acid and good aroma. Some retailers say Brazilian Washed #1 is standard measure for a *neutral* taste. All other coffees are either more or less acid. *Santos* beans, known as *Bourbon*, are the best. They are small, fragrant, make a fair roast with mild, lightly nutty flavor. They may be sharply acid if aged. An official Brazilian publication notes: "Coffee from Minas, classed next to Santos in quality, has a pronounced sourness. Rio coffee, classed #5 has a peculiar, rank flavor and a heavy, harsh taste. It's low price recommends it to packers for their cheapest blends." Brazilian coffees are graded 1, 2, 3, etc., depending on the number of imperfections to each pound. Santos #4 (26 imperfections) is widely used as a standard in international exchange.	

CUSTOM BLENDING

CREATING YOUR OWN BLEND

What can you do with the coffee you have selected? Some commercial roasters say few coffees are so delicious you can't improve them by blending. Conversely, some specialty shop owners will tell you that few blends approach the excellence of pure, unblended coffee.

Fortunately you don't have to choose between them. You can create your own custom blend. Here are some guidelines to start you off.

- Blending equal parts of a good coffee with a poor one produces a mix closest to the poor one.

- Konas blend well with any high grade mild coffees.

- Good Colombias give one-fourth more liquor of a given strength with better flavor than a good grade Brazilian Santos.

- If Colombia or Kona coffees are lighter bodied than you like, enrich them with Kenyan, Sumatran, or Tanzanian coffee.

- Chicory improves any variety.

Your specialty store can also make gourmet blends for you using these formulas:

- Equal parts Java, Mocha, Colombian Excelso

- Equal parts Kona, Mocha, Colombian Excelso

- One-half Kenyan + one-half made up of equal parts of Colombian, Guatemalan, Brazilian, Antiguan.

You can even personalize preferred vacuum packed coffees by blending them with pure coffee from specialty stores.

HOW ROASTS INFLUENCE BLENDS

Roasting develops coffee flavor. The degree of roast changes its taste. Standard roast is mild; French roast, stronger. Explore ways a French roast will affect taste of coffees you like. Consider blending regular roast with French roast, for example. You might like a blend of 1 part French roast Kona with 3 parts regular roast Sumatran for a breakfast coffee you will lick around your mouth all morning long. Then try a blend of half French roast Kona and half regular roast Sumatran for after dinner demitasse.

WHAT SPECIALTY STORES OFFER

Specialty shop owners who roast their own beans or get them frequently from a custom roaster offer a range of roasts not offered in commercial coffees.

Roasting is a highly sensitive, highly skilled craft. The roaster is essentially a revolving cylinder over a gas burner. Custom roasters process 10-25 pounds of green beans at a time at between 300°F and 425°. They use different temperatures for different beans. One man starts a roast with the softer Sumatran beans at about 300°. Then he brings up the heat for other beans as roasting progresses. To compensate for differences in type, age, moisture and size of beans, he roasts different varieties of a blend separately and then blends them.

For dark roasts he uses hard, high grown beans from Peru, Costa Rica, Mexico, El Salvador, Colombia, Kenya and Tanzania. Soft beans would burn up. It takes about 15 minutes, if temperature is right, to roast a batch. If the roaster brings up heat too slowly, beans bake; they don't roast. The principal danger is burning. Full flavor depends on avoiding either under- or overroasting.

When beans reach about 220°, they shrivel, lose moisture and weight. Then they begin to swell to twice their size. Some burst at certain temperatures and you can hear them popping. As beans reach 380°, they are pale brown. At 400° they are medium cinnamon brown. As they reach 425° they are almost black. All this happens quickly and signals the complex inner changes that develop flavor.

All the while the roaster keeps taking samples with a scoop that fits into the roaster to check color of beans by eye and aroma by nose — something a big, computerized machine can't do. It takes years to master this operation.

The minute the beans are done, the roaster stops the process in order to lock in precious volatile oils. Commercial roasters cool beans to room temperature with a spray of cold water and drafts of cold air in the tumbling bin. Some custom roasters use forced air only, saying water quenching accelerates staling.

ONE MAN'S ROASTS

In your search for freshly roasted coffees, be prepared for surprises. We found one small shop in San Francisco's North Beach with only an ancient roaster, a few sacks of green beans, and a counter bare except for a grinder and a cash register. The shop had been there for 40 years.

"What kind of coffee do you sell?" we asked.

"Light roast and dark roast!" was the laconic reply.

"What kind of beans are in your dark roast?" we pursued.

"I blend the best hard beans I can buy. All are hard, clean, high washed, large beans that can take high heat — Altura (Mexican), El Salvador, Colombia, Kenya, Mocha, Sumatra. I use the same blend for light roast. I don't sell 50 varieties. I'd just confuse people," he added gratuitously.

"All those varieties wouldn't sell right away. Some would sit there for days and some would sell at once. If you want good coffee, buy from a house that roasts every day. I roast only 10 pounds at a time with this old machine. All I sell is coffee and do it well."

ADVANTAGES OF DARK ROAST

He had more free advice. "Dark roast removes impurities. I burn out the clinkers and garbage." He took a candy jar from a shelf. "Look at this," he invited.

We saw big flakes of ash, soot, all gray and black. "Where did I get them?" He pointed to a trap in the cooling vent of his roaster.

His views on acidity were unexpected. He dumped a batch of roasted beans into his cooling bin. Smoke gushed a foot high and settled, drawn out by an air vent cooling fan. As he stirred the beans with a big wooden spoon, he said, "The smoke has a lot of the acid and steam in it that we take out in roasting. These are what people say gives coffee a sour taste."

Chemical tests do show that harsh volatile acids in coffee are reduced about 2% in a light roast and about 8% in a dark roast. Also, the darker the roast, the lower the caffeine content.

"Most people think dark roasts produce coffee stronger than light roast," our veteran coffeeman went on. "In one respect, it's the weaker of the two because I remove impurities. So dark roast is light. Compared with commercial brands it has lots more flavor and you use less of it than usual in your coffee maker.

"Those who don't like dark roast say it's overroasted. They say it gives them more strength than flavor, that if you like the taste of slightly burned toast you will like dark roast coffee. I say, try it, you might like it!"

His coffee is good. His customers swear by it.

GRINDING COFFEE

HOW GRINDING UNLOCKS FLAVOR

The minute a green bean is roasted, flavor begins a subtle slide downhill as volatile aromas start dissipating. The aroma loss really accelerates when beans are ground. The finer the grind, the greater the loss. Professional tasters can detect a noticeably stale flavor in samples within a few minutes to a few hours after grinding. Once ground, coffee stays fresh only for a week.

Commercial roasters offer vacuum-pack protection that retains freshness for at least a month. Unfortunately, it often takes up to six weeks to move canned coffee through distribution channels to the front of a grocer's shelves.

Specialty stores encourage customers to buy only small quantities of ground coffee and return often as European shoppers do. Europeans buy four ounces to a half pound at a time, barely enough for 10-25 cups.

Flavor holds up better — up to two weeks — if you buy whole roasted beans. This is why specialty stores urge you to buy whole roasted beans, store them in glass jars sealed with rubber gaskets and grind beans only as needed.

WHAT KIND OF GRIND?

The kind of grind to use varies with the coffee maker. If you like the taste of coffee made with finer grinds than those recommended by the manufacturer, experiment.

Grinding coffee beans yourself is part of the process that makes a cup of coffee a work of art, not just a cup of liquid. The ritual rewards you with a release of aroma that many consider 80 percent of the pleasure of a fine cup. It takes less than two minutes with either hand grinder or electric mill.

Before you buy a grinder that will be best for you, consider the chart of *Features to Look For in a Home Coffee Grinder.*

FEATURES TO LOOK FOR IN A

Electric Grinder/Blender

GRIND SELECTOR Some, but not all blenders will grind coffee. Check manufacturers' instructions. Blades don't grind uniformly. You will get fine and coarse grinds mixed. You must switch off machine when you see coffee is ground as fine as you like.

CAPACITY Some will not grind less than a cup and a half of beans at a time.

CLEANABILITY Easily cleaned by washing in soapy water and rinsing.

CONVENIENCE Takes only seconds. Some require use of separate blender jar. If you own a blender/grinder that operates satisfactorily, do you need a coffee grinder? How often will you use it? Will your blender be more convenient to use, clean and store than a separate coffee grinder?

Electric Blade Type Coffee Grinder

GRIND SELECTOR Most have no setting. You select grind by length of grinding time and stop machine when you see coffee is ground as fine as you want. Takes from 10 seconds for coarse to 25 seconds for fine grind.

CAPACITY Holds enough beans for 6-8 cups coffee.

CLEANABILITY Wipe out with damp cloth. Do not immerse in water.

CONVENIENCE Look for safety control to prevent motor's starting before lid is on. To empty, turn upside down, and pour.

HOME COFFEE GRINDER

Electric Burr Type Coffee Mill

GRIND SELECTOR   Number of graduated settings varies. Some selectors are easier to reach and more specific than others. Best have shiny steel precision balanced burrs that crush and slice beans. Dull, cast iron burrs wear unevenly.

CAPACITY   Varies from 3 ounces to over a pound.

CLEANABILITY   Wipe out collection chamber. Grounds caught in burrs can be dislodged with brush.

CONVENIENCE   Separate collectors for grounds vary in capacity and convenience. It is hard to avoid spillage from almost any kind of grinder. Some models are noisier than others. Check noise level before you buy.

Hand Powered Burr Type Coffee Mill

GRIND SELECTOR   Check the condition and type of burrs and whether you can adjust for different grinds before you buy. Antique models may be more for show.

CAPACITY   Varies. Match mill capacity to capacity of your coffee maker.

CLEANABILITY   Wipe or brush out collection chamber and burrs.

CONVENIENCE   Some are more convenient to operate than others being secured to wall or table with brackets or clamps. Hand grinders require 2-4 minutes physical effort — a definite appeal to ecologists and physical fitness buffs.

A GUIDE TO COFFEE MAKERS
& HOW THEY WORK

Because you can make coffee in many ways, the choice of a coffee maker — or several of them — becomes important.

Some coffee makers become the treasured instruments of the kitchen rituals that wake the day with their lively sounds, invigorating aromas and warming puffs of steam. Some, by their very method, make brewing a little drama you can share with guests. All have advantages and limitations.

You can make excellent coffee in simple, inexpensive pots by just following rules. If you want to expand your coffee repertoire to include brewing styles from around the world, consult this *Guide to Coffee Makers and How They Work* before you shop.

OPEN POT : STEEPING & BOILING METHODS

Steeping has many variations. Bring correct amount of cold water to boil in a pot, kettle or pail and remove from heat. Add ground coffee, stir and cover pot while coffee steeps 2-4 minutes for fine grind; 6-8 minutes for coarse grind. Add small amount of cold water just before serving to settle grounds. To serve, pour coffee through cloth or wire strainer into cups or warmed serving pot.

Advantages: For hundreds of years, the accepted and some say the simplest, foolproof way to brew coffee because you can use almost any grind that is handy

and it doesn't require special pots. Steeping produces mellow, aromatic cup, stronger than drip; not as bitter as percolated. This method is widely used today in Scandinavia where good coffee making is an art.

Limitations: If grounds are not removed from coffee immediately after brewing, coffee becomes bitter from overextraction. Unless carefully poured, grounds get into cups. This may require decanting brew into serving pot.

Boiling also has many variations. Bring water to boil in old fashioned coffee pot or kettle. Add coarse ground coffee and continue boiling 2-5 minutes or longer. Add cold water to settle grounds. Other clarifiers have included eggshells; egg whites, egg, shell and all; fish skin, and salt pork rind.

For Turkish and Arabian method using *ibriks*, see Pages *34-35.*

Advantages: Many people like this strong and bitter coffee and are proud of its cowboy, mud-style, he-man reputation.

Limitations: Coffee is usually cloudy and bitter, even when clarified, for albumin in egg white doesn't coat all fine particles and force them to bottom.

Boiling drives off aromatic, volatile oils and increases caffeine concentration.

FRENCH STYLE PLUNGER POT

Put measured amount of all-purpose or drip grind coffee into tall, heat-resistant glass cylinder. Pour in correct amount of boiling water. Let steep 1-4 minutes, depending on desired strength. Insert plunger with attached perforated metal disk and fine wire screen. Press plunger to bottom through steeped coffee trapping coffee grounds at bottom. Lid that steadies plunger serves as cover. Pour from cylinder to serve.

Advantages: Quickly makes strong, hot coffee fairly free of sediment.

Attractive serving cylinder with built-in steel screen filter makes this unit more convenient than OPEN POT steeping method.

Limitations: Coffee grounds stay at bottom of pot until all coffee is served and pot is emptied.

This is not the kind of pot you put on a warming unit to keep hot.

PORCELAIN DRIP POT

Also called *cafetiere* and dripolator. Pour water that has just come to a boil through porcelain water disperser onto moistened drip grind coffee in removable porcelain section with a fine meshed filter bottom. Brewed coffee drips into pre-heated serving pot.

Advantages: Filtering time is short and makes coffee without metal or paper taste. Small drip grid in filter produces a fairly clear coffee without bitterness.

Permanent porcelain filter is easily cleaned; no paper filters to replace.

Serving pot is elegant accessory and can double as a teapot. Lid that fits top compartments serves as lid for pot. Double handles facilitate removal of drip section.

Limitations: Pot can't be kept warm over direct heat. Heating units must be covered with asbestos pads.

China filter is not as efficient as paper or cloth and coffee can have sediment.

If you are brewing more than a few cups, you must add hot water at intervals to drip section.

NEAPOLITAN FILTER DRIP POT

Pour water into spoutless boiler and slip filter basket sleeve in. Add coffee and screw on perforated lid. Put spouted container on top and place whole unit on heat. When water boils and water spurts from tiny hole at top of boiler, remove from heat, invert pots and allow hot water to filter through coffee into pouring section. Remove boiler and filter sleeve and put lid on serving unit and pour. Or leave units together and serve.

Advantages: Makes strong coffee with some sediment. Small models that make only 2 cups are great for small families.

Limitations: Even with matching heatproof plastic handles, it takes 2-handed dexterity to flip unit over.

There is always a small dribble of water and fear that units will separate in process.

Most units are made of aluminum, a metal that reacts unfavorably with coffee and affects flavor. Units must be scoured after every use.

FILTER DRIP CONE

Pour boiling water into center of funnel shaped filter holder lined with paper filter cone containing very finely ground coffee. Moisten grounds, wait a minute and add rest of boiling water. Coffee filters into server at about a cup a minute. Single pass through of water extracts maximum of flavor without bitterness.

Advantages: Most effective and most recommended method of making mellow coffee free of oils and finest sediment. Depending on your taste, you save money on coffee by using 1 tablespoon instead of the usual 2 to a cup.

Easy to clean; remove messy grounds in filter without soiling hands. Many sizes of inexpensive filter holders available. Laboratory cleanliness and scientific appearance of coffee maker instill feeling of security and expertise.

Limitations: It costs 2-3¢ to replace filters after each use. You must store filter papers with care, for they pick up odors from strongly flavored foods and supplies. These odors and paper taste can affect flavor of coffee. Unit may be hard to pick up if it lacks a handle. Coffee may not be as hot as you like, requiring preheating pot and using serving warmer.

ELECTRIC DRIP FILTER

Cold water, poured into reservoir, is heated to below boiling and dripped over drip grind coffee in a filter basket. Extracted brew enters, at regulated speed, a glass carafe set on a warming plate.

Electric Drip Filter *(continued)*

Advantages: Easy to operate and clean. Makes consistently good, clear brew automatically at a rate of about 1 cup a minute. Experts and users agree all electric drip makers make better coffee than percolators and do it faster and simpler.

Most models are completely automatic and shut off water heating unit at end of brew cycle and switch on warming plate to maintain coffee at correct serving temperature.

Models are more stable than percolators, having larger base.

Filters remove grounds from brew and make disposal easy.

Limitations: *Operating Range.* Not all models deliver strong, flavorful brew when operating at less than full capacity, especially at 1 or 2-cup levels.

Adjust to Taste. Type of grind and proportion to water have to be adjusted to suit your taste and machine's capabilities. If too fine a grind is used, brew may be bitter because of overextraction. If too coarse a grind, coffee will be weak.

Design. Check out several machines before buying. Check if materials used seem flimsy; cup marks hard to read; filter and covers tricky to put in; handles too close to carafe; ON and OFF switches and warning lights present; adequate warranty.

VACUUM SIPHON FILTER

Water in a lower bowl boils and steam forces it up a center spout into an upper bowl. There it bubbles through fine grind coffee. Unit is taken off heat as soon as most of water has risen. As lower bowl cools, a vacuum is created. This pulls brew through a cloth or paper filter into lower bowl in about 3 minutes. Upper bowl containing grounds is removed and coffee is served from lower bowl.

Advantages: Water contacts all coffee fairly rapidly and separates grounds from brew through filter. There is minimum exposure to oxygen to retain natural coffee flavor and aroma; free of sediment.

Chemical laboratory type equipment and exciting visible action have scientific and dramatic appeal.

Pyrex coffee server can be used as teakettle to boil water for other purposes.

Limitations: Removal of hot upper bowl after brewing is difficult, because of tight gripping of rubber gasket and lack of handle, in some cases.

Safety valves and automatic controls lacking. Unit may implode under pressure. Unit must be watched and removed from heat when steam has forced all water into upper bowl. Don't answer phone during this time!! Glass siphon stopper is easily broken.

Warming plate is required to keep coffee hot until served.

To prevent souring, cloth filter must be washed out and kept in cold water between brewings.

PUMPING PERCOLATOR

Water, heated to boiling in bottom of pot is forced up through a pump tube to overflow into a basket holding regular grind coffee. It seeps through and drops into brewed coffee at the bottom. This cycle repeats, circulating brew continually through ground coffee for 6-18 minutes. Remove coffee basket and pour.

In electric models, a thermostat shuts off main heating element when temperature of all the brew nears 200°F. A second element on most percolators keeps coffee warm.

Advantages: Automatic brewing by percolator is a great convenience enjoyed by 86% of Americans. It is a satisfying if not essential morning ritual. Strong smell of coffee and merry chugging sounds and warmth are eye openers hard to give up.

Experts say cup quality is so bad you might as well save money using low grade coffee and not worry whether it is stale or not!

Many models to choose from; wide spread in prices, sizes, materials, speed in brewing, convenience in operation and appearance.

Limitations: Experts say these makers violate good brewing rules. Because brewing time is longer than for drip models, brew is heavy tasting, non-aromatic, oily and often contains sediment. Few have filters.

Many units require removing pump and basket after initial percolation to prevent repercolation. And don't burn your fingers!

Not all models have warning lights to signal end of percolation. Most units hard to clean; should be scoured after each use. Few can be immersed. Special brush needed to clean spout and pump tube.

COLD WATER TODDY

Fit thick felt filter and rubber stopper into receptacles in bottom of steeping bowl. Empty 1 pound regular grind coffee into bowl and add 8 cups cold tap water. Do not stir but push coffee into water until all grounds are moistened.

Leave over night, pull out stopper, place bowl over glass carafe. Coffee drips until carafe is filled in an hour or so.

Place lid on carafe and store in refrigerator; keeps fresh for several weeks, longer if frozen.

Toddy makes a rich, black coffee concentrate. Makes up to 40 cups by simply adding boiling water.

Advantages: You get consistently mellow dark rich fresh-brewed coffee flavor absolutely free of sediment. (Best tasting coffee we've ever had.)

Mix each cup to suit your taste with 1-2 ounces of the concentrate and just add hot water — no waste, no residue. You drink what you make.

No bitterness or oils are released as with high temperature brewing methods.

As quick and easy as instant coffee. For parties you can serve more people than you possibly could with a regular size coffee maker.

Concentrate makes fine essence to add to foods, sauces, iced coffee, other beverages and liqueurs.

Limitations: You must store felt filter in cold water in refrigerator between uses and boil monthly to freshen.

You miss sounds and aromas of the usual coffee making rituals.

ESPRESSO: STEAM ASSISTED FILTER

Machine heats water in pressure boiler in 2-3 minutes and forces boiling water from bottom of boiler through pulverized coffee held in fine-mesh metal filter. Some units have built-in electrical heaters; others are heated on the stove.

Advantages: Espresso method is quick and efficient. All factors affecting good coffee flavor are carefully controlled to produce dark, rich coffee. Many units make steam for frothing milk for cappuccino or heating chocolate and other liquids.

Capacity. You brew cup by cup, not by gallon. No reheating or holding involved.

Far easier to clean than percolators or other makers.

Design. Chrome and stainless steel fittings, plastic knobs, water level gauges, levers and steam tubes delight gadget lovers as much as modern, scientific precision operation.

Limitations: Control knobs in some models are too close to hot surfaces for easy handling.

Check for safety valves, warning lights, OFF and ON switches.

Buy with understanding you can return if there are any leaky valves or fittings.

Units heated on stove must be removed when water has boiled out of base or unit can be ruined.

Most units are more expensive than other types of coffee makers.

While using steam for cappuccino, tube emits a high pitched scream that diminishes to low growl making conversation impossible.

COMPONENTS OF A GOOD CUP OF COFFEE

Brewing Coffee

The search for the coffee you like best naturally ends in your coffee cup. It summarizes all you know about coffee beans, how they are roasted, the ways you can grind them, and what kind of coffee makers and methods will give you the most satisfaction.

What do you assemble to fill your cup? What are the components? They include cup quality, appearance of beans you buy and use, the type of roast, the grind, how you store coffee and even what price you pay.

When you get all this together, you can brew one great cup of coffee after another, time after time.

Here is a chart detailing the components.

1. CUP QUALITY:

CRITERIA	PROFESSIONALS' DESCRIPTIONS	WHAT YOU CAN CHOOSE FOR YOUR CUP
Strength	Pointed Medium Light Lacking	Mild *or* Neutral Mellow *or* Sour Sharp *or* Bitter
Flavor	Fine Good Fair	Sweet *or* Neutral Winy *or* Nutlike Pleasantly sour *or* Earthy
Temperature		Hot *or* Tepid
Body—How it feels in your mouth	Full Light Thin	Full bodied *or* Thin Rich *or* Watery Strong
Aroma	Fine Good Fair	Good Bouquet, High Aroma, Pungence. Tasters check aroma of raw beans, beans hot from roaster, being ground, and being brewed.

2. APPEARANCE OF BEANS:

CRITERIA	PROFESSIONALS' DESCRIPTIONS	WHAT YOU CAN CHOOSE FOR YOUR CUP
Condition	Style	"Style" indicates condition of green or roasted beans. Examine beans for evenness of color, number of defects — black or broken beans, presence of pods, shells, gravel, dirt. Stylish coffee has a good appearance, a look of quality. It roasts evenly.

Size and Shape	Very bold
	Bold
	Medium
	Mixed
	Small
	Peaberries or
	   Caracol
	Elephants
	Quakers (shriveled
	   or undeveloped)
		Size and shape are factors in a good roast. Small hard beans are consistently good roasters. Bigger beans are usually softer and must be watched closely. Small, broken beans and quakers will burn before normal size beans reach full flavor. Elephant beans roast more slowly. Peaberries, being round, roast more evenly than flat beans and bring a premium price.

Color, Raw	Blueish Gray blue Gray green Greenish Grayish Brownish	Some beans change color as they age, decrease in acidity and increase in size. Other beans may mellow with age and gain body and value, depending on storage conditions. Reddish beans often have fermented flavor. Black beans are bad tasting. Older beans tend to be yellowish or tan.
Color, Roasted	Brilliant Bright Ordinary Dull Quakers (off color)	Some coffees roast better than others. Discolored beans produce off flavors. Look for roast of even color, absence of quakers and presence of some white centers. Rough roast has beans varying in size and color.

3. DEGREE OF ROAST:

Note: Coffee beans start to lose flavor and aroma as soon as they are roasted. Get freshly roasted beans, if possible, from a coffeeman who has his own roaster and roasts frequently.

DEGREE OF ROAST	WHAT YOU GET
Light Roast	Beans are cinnamon brown. Light roasts have higher acidity than dark roasts. Roasting reduces caffeine content slightly.
Medium or Straight Roast	These roasts have an even chestnut brown color. Flavor is developed but not to point of bitterness.
Dark or High Roast	Roast uses hard bean coffees. Soft beans can be ruined by a dark roast. Beans are nearly black and develop slightly bitter flavor.
Continental or Vienna Roast*	Lightest of the very dark roasts.
French Roast*	A darker roast that brings oil to surface of beans where it dissipates rapidly. Beans are black.
French Sugar Roast	Sugar added during roasting, caramelizes to make a shiny, oily black bean with bitter flavor.
New Orleans Roast*	Between French and Espresso in darkness. Equally good with or without chicory.
Italian or Espresso Roast*	This roast may be darker than French roast, almost burned. Very strong, bitter flavor. Makes an excellent coffee whether brewed in espresso machines or by other methods suitable for this grind.
Turkish Roast*	One of darkest roasts. Beans are almost burned. (Also Greek, Balkan, Iranian, Cuban, Syrian, Lebanese and Arabian roast.)

Definitions vary. Terms may refer to special blends as well as to degree of roast.

4. GRINDS:

Goal is uniformity of particle size to get best extraction and match kind of grind required by your coffee maker. Every grind contains particles of many sizes but the major portion will match mesh standards for a particular grind. Grinding results depend on degree of roast, hardness, brittleness and moisture content of beans as well as type and grade of coffee. Light roasts do not grind as easily as dark. Dark roasts always give more "fines" than light roasts. Fine grinds release oil more readily and this alters taste.

For best results grind only what you need just before brewing because freshly ground beans stale noticeably within hours. Coarse, medium and fine grinds each have an optimum brewing time. Check your coffee maker for grind that will work best.

GRINDS	DEGREE OF GRIND	EXTRACTION AND EQUIPMENT
Turkish Grind	Pulverized or stone ground	Water and coffee boil up in *ibrik* or saucepan over direct heat in 1-2 minutes.
Espresso Grind	Bordering on powder	Pressurized steam in espresso machine forces hot water through coffee in finely meshed metal filter in 1-2 minutes.
Fine Grind	Less powdery than espresso	Almost boiling water mixes quickly with coffee. Extract is completed in vacuum and some filter pots in 1-4 minutes.
Drip Grind	Small and not large enough to slip through perforations	Quick contact with boiling water in drip and filter pots. For a filter drip, use grind finer than sand. For French drip pot, use grind between drip and regular.
Regular or Coarse Grind	Coarser	Water percolates over grounds in a basket or steeps in open pot 6-8 minutes.
All-Purpose Grind	Mix of coarse, medium and fine	Various

5. STORAGE:

HOW YOU KEEP COFFEE FRESH

Coffee is very perishable. Once beans are roasted, volatile flavors start vanishing. Use beans within three weeks of roasting, ground coffee, within a week.

Store roasted or ground beans in airtight, glass jars in a freezer to retard staling and prevent contamination by other flavors which coffee quickly absorbs. Cans with plastic covers do not provide a secure, protective seal.

Store liquid coffee concentrates in clean, sterile glass jars in refrigerator.

6. PRICE:

WHAT SHOULD YOU PAY?

Price is an indication of quality only up to a point. In June, 1977, the national average price for canned coffee was $3.93 a pound and was estimated to drop 50¢ a pound in 1978. According to knowledgeable merchants, you should be prepared to pay 20-40% more for a selection of top quality coffees in specialty shops. More than that is considered absurd. It is smart to shop. Remember this: if you get 50 cups from a pound of coffee that costs $5.00 or $5.50, you still pay only 10-11¢ a cup.

7. BREWING PROCEDURES:

HOW TO BREW A GREAT CUP OF COFFEE

It is not enough simply to buy high quality coffee beans, roasted to peak of flavor and freshly ground. Help yourself to the best coffee you ever had by observing these procedures.

1. *Use right size coffee maker.* Use a coffee maker big enough to brew the number of cups you plan to serve. Many coffee makers do not perform well at less than three-quarters their capacity. So you won't want to make coffee for two in a pot that makes 12 cups. It helps to have two sizes — one for the family for every day and one for company.

2. *Use scrupulously clean pot.* Even a small amount of stale oil or other residues will adversely affect brewing.

3. *Use pure water.* Water constitutes 99% of the brew. Unless it is pure, it can spoil your coffee. USPH water quality standards require it be tasteless, odorless, colorless and free of bacteria. A little chlorine, organic matter or minerals lower coffee flavor. Alkalinity (hardness) can greatly reduce acid flavor and affect dripping time. Traces of iron or copper affect color and flavor, and also reduce efficiency and life of coffee maker.

   If tap water is hard, highly chlorinated or treated by a water softener, use bottled water.

4. *Measure water accurately.* No guessing, please. Use standard measuring cup and consistently measure correct amount of water for uniform results.

   It's a good idea to check your coffee maker by pouring in the number of 6-ounce cups of water it will hold and still pour well. A 6-cup French drip pot, we find, holds only five 6-ounce cups without spilling. A Neapolitan macchinetta will hold two 6-ounce cups for four 3-ounce servings.

5. *Measure coffee accurately.* Use standard measuring spoon. Use 2 level tablespoons of coffee for each 6-ounce cup of water. Measurement

applies to all drip, vacuum and percolator coffee makers whether electric or not.

Exceptions: Coffee brewed double strength for special recipes; coffee made with Turkish and espresso grinds; coffee made with cold water toddy. Follow instructions that come with your coffee maker, at least the first time. Then adjust to taste.

6. ***Match grind to brewing time.*** No single factor has greater effect on coffee flavor than brewing time. Coarse, medium and fine grinds each have an optimum brewing time and various coffee makers work best with various grinds.

All-purpose grinds combine coarse, medium and fine grinds in an attempt to bracket all coffee makers.

Fine grinds are suited to vacuum and espresso methods with brewing time of 1-4 minutes.

Drip grinds suit drip units with brewing time of 4-6 minutes

Regular or coarse grinds are for percolators, old fashioned pots with brewing time of 6-8 minutes.

Any coffee maker that takes longer than 8 minutes to complete its cycle is overextracting and will produce bitter coffee. If too little time is allowed and water is not hot enough, coffee will be weak.

As soon as brewing is complete, remove spent grounds.

7. ***Use proper water temperature.*** Brew coffee with water just below the boiling point.

8. SERVICE :

HOW TO ENJOY A CUP OF COFFEE

1. ***Serve freshly brewed coffee promptly.*** Brewed coffee can be held for an hour, no longer, at 185°-190°. After that it becomes bitter. If you must reheat coffee, use a double boiler.

2. ***Please your own palate, by all means.*** Serving black coffee is not necessarily the best or most sophisticated way. Black coffee is only an expression of cultural preference. When you use sugar, cream or milk, you simply alter the pH value and taste. These additives dilute and soften flavor, change color and mask aroma.

3. ***Treat coffee as the very adaptable versatile drink it is.*** Add exciting dimensions to its service by brewing it in various ways, serving it in different styles, and offering it in special cups. Alter its strength and flavor to complement companion foods you make and serve with it.

COFFEE COMPANIONS

Ever since coffee became a household beverage, coffee has been going steady with the wholesome and the sweet. A stream of good coffee companions has come out of ovens all over the world — quick breads, yeast breads, rolls, rings, cookies and cakes. Coffee alone can cap a day or a special meal in scores of ways.

SHARING THE WORLD WITH COFFEE

Recipes you find here have been selected because they taste good, because they are fun to make or pretty to see, and because they will send you off on armchair travels at coffeetime.

BREAD CARTE

Begin with the best of coffee companions — bread. Imagine a breakfast like the one Anthony Trollope spread for Plumstead Bishopric in *The Warden*, resplendent with silver coffeepot, cream ewer, sugar bowl and cups of old, dim dragon china and lavish with breads — hot breads and cold, wheaten breads and oaten, white and brown breads, homemade and baker's bread.

You can offer a carte just as imaginative. When you try recipes that follow, use unbleached flour and stone ground whole wheat whenever you can. And don't hesitate to Cornellize or increase the nutritional value of your breads. The formula is simple. For each cup of flour in your recipe, first spoon in 1 tablespoon soy flour, 1 tablespoon skim milk powder, and 1 teaspoon wheat germ and then continue to fill the cup with the required flour.

YEAST BREADS

BREAD IN THE ROUND

This light bodied, delicious whole wheat bread has an ingredients list that is a conversation piece. It can also be a thing of beauty. When loaves are ready for the oven, embellish them by pressing their tops with cookie cutters shaped like shamrocks, diamonds, lambs or other special occasion symbols. Then use a razor or sharp knife to cut the design deep enough to help the dough remember the design during baking.

You can substitute some rye for whole wheat. Bread freezes well.

OMNIBUS WHOLE WHEAT BREAD

1½ cups milk
⅓ cup light salad oil
2 tablespoons molasses
2 tablespoons honey
2 teaspoons salt

½ cup warm water
2 tablespoons yeast
¼ cup chopped almonds
¼ cup sunflower seeds
2 tablespoons sesame seeds
1 tablespoon caraway seeds
2 tablespoons wheat germ

2 cups whole wheat flour
4½ cups white flour

Glaze: 1 egg beaten with 1 tablespoon water and
½ teaspoon brown sugar

Scald milk and stir in oil, molasses, honey and
salt. Cool to lukewarm. Put warm water in large
warm bowl and sprinkle yeast over it. Stir until
dissolved. Add lukewarm milk mixture, nuts,
seeds, wheat germ, whole wheat and 1 cup white
flour. Beat until smooth.

Add enough flour to make stiff dough and turn
out and knead until smooth and elastic, about 10
minutes. Put in buttered bowl to rise in warm
place until double in bulk, about 1 hour. Punch
down, divide in two and shape round loaves.
Place on buttered, round 8-in. cake tins. Let rise
in warm place until double. Decorate surface
with cutters and sharp knife and bake at 375° for
30-35 minutes. Glaze and remove from pans to
cool on wire racks.

Serve with a flourish of trumpets!

Yield: 2 loaves

TO MAKE A BANQUET, ADD BUTTER

This fragrant bread owes its delicate sweetness to
maple syrup. It has excellent texture and sets a fine
brown crust. It makes delicious, chewy toast.

OATMEAL BREAD

1 cup regular oatmeal
2 cups boiling water
½ cup maple syrup
1 tablespoon salad oil
1 tablespoon yeast dissolved in
    ¼ cup lukewarm water
1 teaspoon salt
5 cups white flour

Pour boiling water over oatmeal and cool to
lukewarm. Add syrup, oil and dissolved yeast.
Stir in 2 cups flour and hold in warm place until
sponge has risen once and fallen slightly. Beat in
salt and remaining flour. Turn out and knead for
10 minutes until smooth and elastic. Place dough
in buttered bowl and let rise 35-40 minutes until
double. Divide dough to make two loaves. Place
in buttered loaf pans and let rise again until
double, about 30 minutes. Bake 10 minutes at
375°. Reduce heat to 350° and continue baking
30-40 minutes. Cool on rack.

Yield: 2 loaves

Bring whole loaves to coffee table and let guests
cut their slices. Serve with sweet butter.

MAKE IT BEAUTIFUL

Bake this cocoa bread in a bundt pan. It cuts to a
pinkish brown and has a very light, fine texture.
Chocolate taste wants nothing to complete it but
sweet butter.

COCOA BREAD

1 tablespoon yeast
2 cups milk, scalded and cooled
2 beaten eggs
¾ cup sugar
½ teaspoon salt
½ cup cocoa
¼ cup salad oil
6 cups white flour

Dissolve yeast in warm milk. Beat in 3 cups flour to make smooth batter and let rise in warm place. When batter is light, add eggs, sugar sifted with cocoa and salt, oil and remaining flour. Knead lightly and put in buttered bowl to rise until double, about 2 hours. Knead again. Put dough in well buttered bundt pan. Let rise until double. Bake at 400° for 50 minutes or until done.

Yield: 1 large bundt loaf

A SCANDINAVIAN SPECIAL

Americans may buy more coffee than Scandinavians, but Scandinavians drink more coffee per capita. They make excellent breads for coffee companions.

Here is a recipe for beautiful Swedish rye. If our Erika were making it, she would turn up the hi-fi with the Beach Boys' *Help Me Rhonda*. It lasts just long enough and has the right rhythm to make kneading fun for ten minutes. Serve plain with butter or soft cream cheese and orange marmalade.

SWEDISH RYE BREAD

2 cups rye flour
½ cup soy flour
5 cups white flour

½ cup brown sugar
1 teaspoon salt
2 teaspoons caraway seeds
½ teaspoon crushed anise seeds
Grated rind of 1 orange

2 tablespoons yeast
2 cups hot tap water
⅓ cup molasses
2 tablespoons softened margarine

In a large warm bowl combine and thoroughly mix flours. Using 2½ cups of this mix, add sugar, salt, caraway, anise, orange rind and stir in yeast. Slowly add hot water and beat 2 minutes — at medium speed if using an electric mixer.

Add molasses, margarine and another cup of flour mix. Beat vigorously for 2 minutes. Stir in enough additional flour to make a dough you can knead. Knead until smooth, about 10 minutes. Place in buttered bowl and let rise in warm place until double, about 1 hour. Punch down, divide into 2 balls. Place on buttered cookie sheet or round cake tins. Slash dough diagonally with a sharp knife. Let rise in warm place until double, another hour or so.

Bake at 375° for 40 minutes. Turn out on cooling rack and glaze still hot loaves with 2 tablespoons milk mixed with 1 teaspoon brown sugar. Beautiful! Yield: 2 round loaves

MAKE A BASKETFUL OF RAISIN BREADS

Here are three raisin breads you can bake and freeze and effortlessly display for afternoon coffee. They range from white to dark and want nothing but butter.

First is a French version of an Irish bread. In Ireland the bread traditionally conceals a ring, silver coin and button to tell fortunes. If you get the ring, you will marry; the coin, you will be rich; the button, you will remain single! If you add this Irish flummery, wrap items in foil before adding to the dough so that guests won't have to swallow them, too!

FRENCH BARMBRACK

4 cups flour
½ teaspoon salt
½ cup shortening

1 scant tablespoon yeast
½ cup sugar
2 cups lukewarm non-fat milk
2 well beaten eggs
½ cup currants
½ cup sultanas
2 tablespoons chopped citron

Sift flour with salt into mixing bowl. Using blending fork rub in shortening until there are no lumps. Mix yeast thoroughly with sugar and add milk. Pour milk mix into flour mix, add eggs. Beat until smooth. Cover bowl and put in warm place to rise for 1½ hours. Add fruits. Divide dough between 2 well buttered loaf tins and let rise again for 20 minutes. Bake at 350° for 30 minutes.   Yield: 2 loaves

Next is a light textured brown bread made with firm apples and raisins.

RAISIN-APPLE BREAD

2 tablespoons yeast
½ cup warm water
1 cup scalded milk
3 tablespoons honey
1 teaspoon salt
1 beaten egg
½ cup rye flour
1½ cups whole wheat
1 cup seedless raisins
1 cup chopped apples
3 cups white flour

Glaze: 1 egg yolk beaten with 1 teaspoon milk

Dissolve yeast in water. Cool scalded milk to lukewarm and add yeast mix, honey and salt. Slowly pour mix into beaten egg. Stir in rye, whole wheat, raisins and apples. Knead in white flour, working dough until smooth. Set in buttered bowl to rise until double. Punch down, form two loaves and place in buttered loaf pans to rise again for 45 minutes. Glaze loaves and bake at 350° for 35-40 minutes. If tops brown too fast, cover with aluminum foil until loaves are baked.   Yield: 2 loaves

The third bread has a secret ingredient. Few will guess what it is until you tell them. It is chicory, the same you buy to make your coffee just a bit better. You can make the essence by soaking ground chicory root which you buy at specialty coffee shops, and straining liquid through a fine sieve. The loaves are rather flat but the bread has soft body, good crust and a rich caramellike flavor. Darkest of the raisin breads, it is delicious with *café au lait*. Spread it with butter or a triple crême cheese.

CHICORY RAISIN BREAD

2 tablespoons yeast
½ teaspoon sugar
½ cup warm water

1 cup warm chicory essence
3 tablespoons butter
1 teaspoon salt
¼ cup dark molasses
1 cup raisins
1 beaten egg
2 cups pumpernickel flour
1 cup whole wheat
1 cup white flour

Dissolve yeast in water and sugar. Heat chicory essence and add butter, salt, molasses, raisins and egg. Combine two mixes and stir into pumpernickel and whole wheat. Mix well. Knead in white flour. Only a mother could love this dough, it's so stubborn and tough to work, but stay with it until you have a smooth mass, about 10 minutes. Place in buttered bowl in warm place to rise until double. Be patient. This may take a couple of hours. Don't be stampeded into hurrying process. Punch down and knead briefly. Form two loaves and place in buttered loaf pans to rise until double. Bake at 350° for 30 minutes or until done.   Yield: 2 loaves

QUICK BREADS

EASY DOES IT

Even unexpected guests present no real problem. Simply make conversation while you make and bake a quick bread. To make it easy, keep your pantry stocked with nuts, spices, baking powder, soda, currants, raisins, honey, molasses, sugars and interesting flours. Try these.

BE FRENCH!

This spongy bread is sweet and elegantly French. Serve this coffee companion unadorned, thinly sliced.

FRENCH HONEY BREAD

1 cup honey
½ cup sugar
1 cup milk
2 egg yolks, beaten
2½ cups flour sifted with
　　1 teaspoon soda
　　½ teaspoon salt

Combine honey, sugar and milk in saucepan and heat slowly, stirring constantly. Cool. Add yolks and stir in dry ingredients gradually to prevent lumping of batter. Divide batter between two small loaf pans lined with buttered waxed paper. Bake at 325° for 1½ hours. Remove from pans and cool on rack. Voilà!
          Yield: 2 small loaves

BE HEALTHY!

Silvester Graham, early 19th Century American doctor, gets as much notice in Webster's *Pronouncing Biographical Dictionary* as George III of England. No wonder, he is father of the flour that makes the next bread so wholesome. It is very easy to make; freezes well. Bake the batter in empty soup cans and bring neat little round slices to the coffee table.

AUNT KATY'S HEALTH BREAD

2 cups bran
2 cups Graham flour
1 cup rye flour
2 teaspoons soda
Pinch of salt
1 cup light molasses
1½ cups buttermilk

Mix all together until damp. Pour batter into 6 well buttered soup cans, filling cans only half full and bake at 350° for 45 minutes.

Yield: 6 small loaves

BE INVENTIVE!

Various versions of this good coffee cake call for filberts and coconut; cinnamon and almonds; or cocoa and walnuts. So you can use what you happen to have and improvise the first four ingredients.

COCOA COFFEE CAKE

½ cup sugar
1 teaspoon cinnamon
1 tablespoon cocoa
½ cup chopped walnuts

½ cup butter
1 cup sugar
3 beaten eggs
3 cups flour sifted with
   1 teaspoon baking soda
   3 teaspoons baking powder
1¼ cups sour cream

Combine first 4 ingredients and set aside.

Cream butter until light and slowly add sugar. Beat eggs in one at a time. Add flour mixture

alternately with sour cream. Spoon one half the batter into 9-inch tube or bundt pan that has been well buttered and dusted with flour. Sprinkle half the cinnamon mix over batter. Cover with remaining batter and sprinkle on last of cinnamon mix.

Bake at 350° for 40-50 minutes. Cool on rack for 10 minutes before turning out of pan.

Yield: 1 large coffee cake

ROLLS & OTHER EXTRAVAGANCES

Delicious things happen when you make rolls and buns, braids and rings and when you imitate the Greeks and South Americans and make coffee companions by the panful. And who doesn't dream of bearing in a tray of fresh baked croissants for morning coffee?

Let's start with homely stuff with a superior crust. Pepper heightens the cheese flavor and you can form the dough in any shape you like — round, oval, muffin, ring or braid.

TINA'S PEPPER ROLLS

4½ cups of flour
2 tablespoons yeast
1 cup milk
½ cup water
¼ cup shortening
2 tablespoons sugar
1½ teaspoons salt
2 teaspoons freshly ground pepper
1 room temperature egg
2 cups shredded sharp cheddar cheese

Sprinkle yeast over 1¾ cups flour in large bowl and stir to mix. Combine milk, water, shortening, sugar, salt and pepper in saucepan and heat until warm. Pour this into flour and yeast mix and add egg. Beat 30 seconds with electric beater at low speed, then 3 minutes at high speed.

Stir in cheese and remaining flour by hand to make soft dough. Turn out on floured board and knead until smooth. Cover dough and let rise for 20 minutes in warm place. Shape rolls and place in well buttered muffin tins or on buttered baking sheet to rise until double, about 40 minutes. Bake at 375° for 15-20 minutes. Brush with butter and serve.

Yield: 3 dozen rolls

ONLY THE SHAPE IS TURKISH

Greeks make a very tasty crescent with sesame seeds. Start with all ingredients at room temperature.

GREEK CRESCENTS

4 cups flour
2 tablespoons yeast
2 well beaten eggs
½ teaspoon salt
⅓ cup sugar
½ cup melted shortening
½ cup warm water to make soft dough
Sesame seeds for sprinkling

Glaze: 1 egg yolk mixed with 1 teaspoon water.

Place all ingredients except water and sesame seeds in bowl. Add water a little at a time until

you have a soft dough. Set aside to rise in warm place.

Roll dough out ½ inch thick. Cut into strips and then into triangles. Roll into crescents, starting from wide end of triangles. Pull ends together to form crescent and place on buttered sheet to rise. Brush with glaze and sprinkle with sesame and bake at 375° for 10 minutes. Serve hot or cold.

Yield: 4 dozen small rolls

FROM THE BAKER'S BAKER

This recipe produces sheer delight. With it we make everything from elaborate coffee rings to artless little buns baked in muffin tins, as Aunt Edie intended.

EDIE'S DELICATE ROLLS

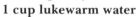

1 tablespoon yeast
1 cup lukewarm water
1 tablespoon sugar
1 cup scalded milk
6 cups flour
1 beaten egg
4 tablespoons shortening, softened
3 tablespoons sugar
1 teaspoon salt

Glaze: 1 egg beaten with 3 tablespoons powdered sugar and 1 tablespoon water.

Combine first 3 ingredients, stir and let stand 10 minutes. Scald milk and cool. Add to yeast mix and stir in half the flour, beating until smooth. Add egg, shortening, sugar, salt and remaining flour. Knead into a medium firm dough, adding more flour if necessary until dough is smooth and elastic. Let dough rise until double. Knead down and let rise again until about ¾ the size of first rising. Punch down and shape rolls as desired. Easiest is to roll into balls and set to rise in well buttered muffin tins until double. Bake at 400° for 20 minutes. Remove from tins, brush with glaze while still hot and serve with butter only.

Yield: 3 dozen +

FROM A VERY FAMOUS CONTRIBUTOR

The most famous of them all, Anonymous, contributed this recipe. It is handwritten on a 3×5 card yellowed with age. Too bad, because it makes the most delicately textured coffee bread of all. When you send your best recipe to a friend, for goodness' sake, date it and sign your name. Never go unsung like this! You can use this basic dough for other sweet rolls. Variations follow for other fillings.

ORANGE ROLLS

3 eggs
½ cup sugar
1 cup milk
3 tablespoons butter
1 tablespoon yeast
½ teaspoon salt
4 cups flour
Grated rind of 1 lemon

Filling: Combine ¼ cup melted butter, ½ cup sugar and grated rind of 1 orange.

Beat eggs slightly and add sugar. Scald milk and add butter. When lukewarm, add yeast and salt. Add to egg mixture and mix well. Beat in 1 cup of flour and set batter aside to rise in warm place, about 1 hour.

Add remaining flour and grated lemon and stir but do not knead. Let rise for about 2 hours. When dough is light, roll it out on floured board and spread with filling. This is a very delicate dough and requires patience. Roll up as you would cinnamon rolls, cut off pieces and place cut side down in well buttered muffin tins. Let rise in warm place for about 2 hours. Bake at 375° for 15 minutes. Remove from pans immediately and serve hot with butter.

Yield: 30 rolls

VARIATIONS

Pecan Rolls

Filling: Cream 2 tablespoons butter, 1 teaspoon cinnamon and ½ cup brown sugar.

Topping: Cream ¼ cup butter and ⅓ cup brown sugar and spoon into buttered muffin tins, finishing off with a few pecans. Place rolled, filled rolls on top. Bake at 350° 15-18 minutes. Serve upside down.

Poppyseed and Honey Rolls

Filling: Combine ½ cup poppyseeds, ¼ cup soft butter, 2 tablespoons honey, ½ cup coarsely chopped walnuts, grated rind of 1 orange. Brush risen rolls with egg yolk beaten with milk and bake at 350° for 25 minutes.

FROM A KANSAS GRANDMOTHER

Grandmother's cookbook has marvelous coffee companions with amusing names like this one. The uncut original recipe would feed an army. This dough is a slow riser. Be patient.

SNAIL HOUSE CAKES

3 cups flour
¾ cup sugar
½ cup soft butter
4 eggs
1½ tablespoons yeast
½ cup raisins
½ cup currants
½ cup finely chopped almonds
2 tablespoons finely chopped citron

Thoroughly mix half the flour, half the butter, half the sugar and 4 eggs and add yeast. Set aside to rise. When batter is light, add remaining flour and knead until smooth. Roll dough out into a rectangle ¼ inch thick. Cut into strips 2 inches wide and 8-10 inches long. Brush with remaining butter and lay on fruit, remaining sugar, nuts and citron. Roll each strip separately and lay close together on buttered baking sheet. Let rise again until double and bake at 350° for 15 minutes.

Yield: 12 large cakes

DOWN SOUTH OF THE BORDER

This Mexican sweet roll spices coffeetime with cinnamon and cocoa.

MEXICAN SWEET ROLLS

¾ cup scalded milk
½ cup sugar
1 teaspoon salt
½ cup shortening
½ cup warm water
2 tablespoons yeast
1 egg
4½ cups flour

Filling: Combine ¼ cup soft butter, 1 tablespoon cinnamon, 2 tablespoons cocoa, 2 tablespoons finely chopped almonds and ⅓ cup sugar.

Add sugar, salt and shortening to scalded milk. Pour warm water into large warm bowl and sprinkle yeast over it. Stir until dissolved. Add milk mix cooled to lukewarm, egg and half the flour. Beat until smooth. Stir in enough remaining flour to make stiff dough and knead until smooth. Place in buttered bowl, cover tightly and refrigerate for 2 hours.

Divide dough in two and roll out each half to a large square. Spread dough with filling. Cut dough in 3-inch squares, fold opposite ends to middle and secure with beaten egg. Place on buttered baking sheet and let rise in warm place until double. Brush with beaten egg and bake at 375° for 12-15 minutes. Remove from pan and cool on rack.

Yield: 3 dozen rolls

WHAT IS IT?

What is as American as apple pie and has been popular in Greece since the 5th Century B.C.? Swedes make it with rye and white flour, orange juice, powdered fennel and brown sugar. Dutch make it plain. French flavor it with vanilla. Old American recipes make hearty use of nutmeg. Turks soak it in syrup, sprinkle it with hazelnuts and smother it with whipped cream.

A cake or a bread? The dictionary says it is both. It is rusk, the twice baked cookie. Here are two European versions.

GREEK RUSKS

1 cup butter
1 cup sugar
3 eggs
1 teaspoon crushed anise seeds
¼ cup sesame seeds
2½ cups flour sifted with
   3 teaspoons baking powder
   ⅛ teaspoon salt

Cream butter and sugar thoroughly. Add eggs one at a time, then seeds, blending well. Add dry ingredients. Spoon batter into small, well buttered loaf pans (3) and bake at 350° for about 35 minutes. Cool on rack.

Toasting: Cut loaves in ½-inch slices and place on unbuttered baking sheet. Bake at 250° for about 40 minutes. Turn pieces once during this time. Cool and store in tightly closed tin. Serve plain with coffee.

Yield: 40 rusks

A FAVORITE DUNKER

While Greek rusks are softly crisp, the Italian rusk is rock hard. Dunked, it quickly becomes chewable and adds spicy aroma to give a cup of coffee a delicate dimension.

ANISE RUSKS

3 cups flour sifted with
   1 cup sugar
   1 tablespoon baking powder
   ½ teaspoon salt
Grated rind of 1 lemon
2 teaspoons crushed anise seed

4 well beaten eggs
2 tablespoons cream
1 cup finely chopped almonds

Sift dry ingredients into a bowl and mix in lemon rind, anise, eggs, cream and nuts to make a firm dough. Pack into 3 small, well buttered loaf pans lightly dusted with flour. Bake at 350° for 30 minutes. Cool on racks. Follow the same toasting procedure as for Greek Rusks.

Yield: 4 dozen

SOUTH AMERICAN PAN PARAISO

"Paradise bread" lives up to its name. You can make it as sweet as you like. Fruit topping sinks into a soft, briochelike dough. Bread has a deliciously crusty bottom. Freezes well.

PAN PARAISO

1 cup hot milk
⅓ cup butter
¼ cup sugar
½ teaspoon salt
1 tablespoon yeast dissolved in
   ¼ cup lukewarm milk
1 well beaten egg
2¾ cups flour

Topping: Fresh apples, sugar and cinnamon for sprinkling, 1 egg yolk beaten with 3 tablespoons cream.

Add butter, sugar and salt to hot milk. When mixture is lukewarm, add dissolved yeast, egg and flour to make stiff batter. Cover and let rise 1 hour.

Roll out dough as thin as possible to cover bottom of well buttered cookie sheet. Cover and let rise again. Core, peel and slice apples in crescents and lay on dough close together in neat little rows. Sprinkle with mixed sugar and cinnamon. Drizzle egg and cream mix around apples. Bake at 375° for 20 minutes or until crust is well baked and fruit is soft. (Peaches, plums, apricots or nectarines may be substituted for apples.) Cut in serving pieces and serve this very stylish bread hot with coffee.

Yield: 15 generous servings

PHENOMENA AND FOLKLORE

A Finnish proverb states: If bubbles rise on the surface of your coffee and hold together, good weather is in store. If bubbles burst, weather will be bad!

All this because a farmer probably dropped a few lumps of sugar in his breakfast coffee and saw little bubbles jumping in the air. In the fields that day, he observed rain and wind. When the same things happened repeatedly, the farmer matched coffee bubbles with bad weather. As simple as that. Whatever the weather, he could enjoy coffee braids with rich crust and fine texture and forget the message of the bubbles in his cup.

FINNISH COFFEE BRAIDS

2 eggs
1 cup lukewarm milk
¾ cup brown sugar
1 teaspoon salt
1 teaspoon freshly ground cardamom
1 tablespoon yeast dissolved in
   ½ cup lukewarm water

2 cups light rye flour
3¾ cups white flour
½ cup melted butter

Glaze: Mix well 1 egg, 3 tablespoons sugar and 2 tablespoons water.

Thoroughly beat eggs into milk. Add sugar, salt and cardamom, then dissolved yeast. Beat in rye and add white flour to make soft dough. Turn out and knead well. Add butter and mix thoroughly. Cover and let rise in warm place until double. Knead again and let rise. When dough is doubled, knead down and divide into 6 equal parts. Roll each piece into a strip about 18 inches long. Use 3 for each braid. Braid strands and place on well buttered round cake tins. Let rise until double. Bake at 375° for 10 minutes. Reduce heat to 350° and continue baking 30 minutes. Glaze braids as soon as you take them from the oven. Cool on rack.

Yield: two 8-inch braids

VIVE LA FRANCE!

One of the delicious experiences you bring home from a French bakery or from France is the eating of croissants with breakfast coffee. In France the bakery does it all. Few housewives take on the job when the bakery is so handy and does such a fine job. Here at home, you have to fend for yourself or do without.

More pastry than bread, croissants originated in 17th Century Budapest. The French added laurels by putting them very high on the list of good things to eat with morning coffee.

CROISSANTS

½ cup milk
2 teaspoons sugar
1 tablespoon shortening

½ teaspoon yeast
1 teaspoon sugar
¼ cup lukewarm water

1 beaten egg
1 teaspoon grated lemon rind
2½ cups flour (or enough for soft dough)

½ cup butter
1 egg beaten with
    1 tablespoon cream

Scald milk and add sugar and shortening. Cool to lukewarm. Dissolve yeast and sugar in water and let stand 10 minutes. Add to milk mixture. Add egg, lemon rind and flour to make soft dough. Knead until elastic and place in buttered bowl to rise in warm place until double.

Prepare butter by shaping it into a rectangle, mixing in a little flour to keep it from sticking and placing it between sheets of waxed paper dusted with flour. Roll out ¼ inch thick and cut in two. Wrap halves separately in waxed paper and chill.

Roll dough out on floured board to rectangle 3 times longer than wide. Dust off excess flour and place half the butter in center of rectangle. Fold right end over butter and place second half on top and fold left end over butter. Pinch edges together to seal in butter layers.

Place the folded dough on the lightly floured board so that you are facing the short end and roll dough into original rectangle. Brush off any excess flour and again fold dough, this time with each flap meeting in the middle and another time so that the dough folds from the middle like a book. Wrap dough and chill for 1 hour.

Return dough to floured board and repeat rolling and folding. Chill again for several hours.

Divide dough in half, keeping 1 piece refrigerated while you roll out the other to a rectangle ⅛ inch thick. Cut strips and divide into triangles. Brush points with egg and cream and roll up triangles from wide end. Chill 30 minutes, pull shaped rolls into crescents and place on buttered baking sheet to rise until double. Brush with egg and cream mix and bake at 400° for 15 minutes, then at 350° until golden.

Yield: 18 rolls

SOME FABULOUS THINGS

Some of life's most precious memories are of things that excite slight notice in the world — a Grandmother's cake, an Aunt's brownies — things wrapped in the good times you had with the maker. Some are simply discoveries and awakening realization that what you have found, you can somehow learn to make.

A VERY SPECIAL SPICE CAKE

Here is one that has an affectionate original name for a Grandmother because some small child couldn't say the word.

GOGAYE'S SPICE CAKE

1 cup sugar
Butter the size of an egg
1 egg
1 cup sour cream or buttermilk
1 cup flour sifted with
    1 scant teaspoon soda
    1 teaspoon baking powder
    1 teaspoon each: cinnamon, cloves and
    allspice
Handful of raisins

Cream butter and sugar. Add egg and beat well.
Add sour cream and flour mix alternately, then
raisins. Pour batter into 9-inch square pan that
has been buttered and dusted with flour. Bake at
350° for 30 minutes.

Yield: 9 servings

THANK YOU, AUNT AGNES!

This brownie appeared at a big family gathering
in Michigan. Aunt Agnes found it necessary to rap
wrists if she left the panful unguarded even for a
minute. We honestly thought she would never give
us the recipe, but here it is. It makes a big batch.

AUNT AGNES' BROWNIES

Melt 1 cup butter with 3 squares of chocolate and
blend with 2 cups sugar, 1 teaspoon salt or less
and 4 eggs. Stir 1 cup flour and 2 cups walnuts in
and add 2 teaspoons vanilla. Pour into buttered
cookie sheet (10 × 16) with sides. Bake at 325° for
30-35 minutes or until edges pull away from pan.
Cool in pan and frost.

Frosting: Beat 1 egg well and gradually work in 1
pound of sifted powdered sugar. Melt ¼ pound
of butter with 1 square bitter chocolate and add
to sugar. Add 1 teaspoon vanilla and 2
tablespoons cream. Mix well and spread over
cooled brownies.

Yield: 40 two-inch squares

LEGENDARY FRENCH COOKIE

In Dumas' *Grand Dictionnaire de Cuisine* a hungry
traveler finds a bakery lit by an immense oven and
operated by a man of ferocious mien but hospitable
instincts. He offers the stranger a basket filled with
little shell-like cakes, "Taste these and tell me what
you think."

The guest eats them all with relish and asks,
"What do you call these succulent dainties?"

They are the still famous *madeleines de Commercy.*
Make them in madeleine molds if you can. If you
can't, bake them in a sheet and cut diamond shapes
to serve.

MADELEINES

1 cup sugar
4 eggs
Pinch of salt
1 teaspoon grated lemon rind
2 cups sifted pastry flour
1 cup butter, melted and cooled
Additional butter for brushing molds.

In a bowl beat sugar and eggs until light. Blend
in salt and lemon rind. Fold in flour and butter.
Do not beat. Fill well buttered, flour dusted
madeleine molds ⅔ full and bake at 375° for
15-20 minutes.

Yield: 40 +

A GREAT DANE

One of the cakes most often on Danish coffee tables is sand cake. You bake it in a sheet. The only offbeat ingredient is potato flour. Buy this in health food stores.

SAND CAKE

1 cup sugar
1½ cups butter
6 eggs separated
1 cup potato flour sifted with
    2 cups white flour
1 teaspoon vanilla

Thoroughly cream butter and sugar. Add egg yolks, one at a time, beating well after each addition. Add flour and vanilla, mixing well. Fold in stiffly beaten egg whites. Pour dough into well buttered, flour dusted 13×9×2½ cake pan and bake at 350° for about 30 minutes. Serve plain, cut in squares.

Yield: 24 servings

A DECEPTIVE SCANDINAVIAN

Never serve sandbakkels next to creamed turkey! Our Man once mistook them for patty shells, spooned creamed turkey into them. What a droll fate for a Scandinavian cookie!

With admirable aplomb he ate the mistake with enthusiasm and went back for more. The second time, he followed a roomful of Norwegian advisers and filled the cookie with whipped cream and jam.

Sandbakkels are baked in pretty little metal molds. You press chilled dough into them and bake them in the molds. You serve them upside down so the pattern shows; or turn them right side up to make little dishes to be filled with jam.

SANDBAKKELS

1 cup butter
1 cup sugar
2 eggs
¼ teaspoon almond extract
2¾ cups flour
⅓ cup finely chopped blanched almonds

Cream butter and sugar adding sugar gradually. Add eggs and beat well. Add almond extract, then flour and almonds. Mix well. Chill dough ½ hour.

Traditionally, bakers press dough into molds. We find it easier to roll out small sections of dough to a uniform thinness and then press dough into molds. Whatever you do, keep dough well chilled.

Place molds on cookie sheets and bake at 375° for 6-8 minutes or until golden. Remove from oven and place on smooth board upside down. Cookies will fall out of molds as they cool. They freeze well.

Yield: 4 dozen

FESTIVE RUM BABAS

That passionate cook, King Stanislas, invented these exotic little cakes. They say he called them babas in tribute to Ali Baba. But the Ukrainians tell you that baba is a common word for woman or grandma and they have a long, involved explanation worth exploring, and their breads and cakes are fabulous.

BABAS AU RHUM

1 teaspoon sugar
⅓ cup lukewarm water
2 tablespoons yeast

½ cup scalded milk cooled to lukewarm
½ cup flour
1 teaspoon salt
5 eggs
½ cup sugar
⅓ cup melted butter
Grated rind of 1 lemon
½ teaspoon cardamom
About 3 cups flour

Rum syrup: Boil ½ cup water with 1 cup sugar for 10 minutes. Cool. Add 1 teaspoon lemon juice and ¼ to ½ cup of rum.

Dissolve sugar in water and sprinkle yeast over it. Let stand 10 minutes. Combine with milk and ½ cup flour. Beat thoroughly and set aside in warm place until light and bubbly. Add salt to eggs and beat well. Beat in sugar and stir in remaining ingredients except flour. Add egg mix to sponge and beat in remaining flour until you have a smooth thick batter. Cover and let rise until double. Punch down and let rise again.

If you do not have individual baba molds, use fruit cans (8½ oz. size). Butter cans and fill ½ full and set to rise double in warm place. Bake at 350° for 10 minutes, reduce heat to 325° and continue baking until inserted toothpick comes out clean. Pour rum syrup over babas while they are still warm. Place on large serving plate and let guests help themselves. They freeze well.

Yield: 10-12 babas

DESSERTING COFFEE

Coffee is essential to many dessert drinks with toppings, spices, various seasonings and with or without spirits. Some are classics. Some appear during winter holidays and are good on any cold night. Some bow to national tastes and cultural preferences. Use preheated cups for all hot drinks.

NONALCHOLIC

AMERICAN

Measure water for number of cups to be served. For each cup add ½ inch stick cinnamon, 3 whole cloves, 2 allspice berries. Bring to boil in saucepan and simmer 10 minutes. Strain and add water if necessary. Brew coffee in regular way, using spiced water. Serve in mugs topped with sweetened whipped cream or vanilla ice cream.

BELGIAN

Beat 2 egg whites stiff and fold in 2 cups sweetened whipped cream flavored with vanilla. Half fill cups with this meringue and complete cups with strong, hot coffee. Serve at once. Serves 6.

BRAZILIAN

Melt and blend 2 squares bitter chocolate with 1 cup strong coffee in a double boiler. Add pinch of salt and 2 tablespoons sugar. Boil 4 minutes, stirring constantly. Add 3 cups milk and continue stirring. When it is hot, beat to a froth with eggbeater or whisk. Cool. Pour over cracked ice in tall glasses and top with 1 tablespoon sweetened whipped cream. Serves 4.

CAFFÈ BORGIA

Pour equal parts of hot chocolate and strong coffee into cups. Top with sweetened whipped cream and sprinkle with grated orange peel and shaved sweet chocolate.

CUBAN

Combine 3 cups light cream and 1 cup finely ground coffee in a saucepan and simmer 5 minutes. Strain through fine sieve and pour into cups. Top with whipped cream and serve with sugar. Serves 4.

DUTCH

In each cup of hot black coffee, place a cinnamon stick and 1 tablespoon heavy cream and stir. Float a pat of sweet butter on top.

HAWAIIAN

Scald 2 cups milk and add 1 cup shredded coconut and 2 tablespoons sugar. Refrigerate over night. Strain and reheat in double boiler. Add 2 cups strong hot coffee and serve topped with toasted coconut. Serves 6.

INDIA COFFEE

Use 1 tablespoon finely ground mocha for each cup. Bring water to boil, add coffee, stirring constantly. For each 4 cups, add 1 tablespoon rose water and serve plain in demitasse.

INDIAN JASMINE COFFEE

For each serving, combine ½ cup water, 1 crushed cardamom seed and ½ teaspoon jasmine tea. Bring to boil and set aside at once, tightly covered, to steep 2 minutes. Strain into standard cup or glass, filling only half. Add to each cup ⅓ cup prepared espresso and stir in 1 teaspoon sugar. Top with whipped cream.

MEXICAN

Whip ½ cup whipping cream with ¼ teaspoon each of nutmeg and cinnamon. Spice 1½ cups strong black coffee with ½ teaspoon cinnamon and sweeten to taste. Serve demitasse with generous spoonful of the whipped cream. Serves 4.

PUNCH

Steep for 15 minutes over low heat 2 quarts strong hot coffee, peels of 1 orange and 1 lemon cut in strips, 4 cinnamon sticks, 1 teaspoon whole cloves, ⅓ cup sugar, ¼ cup chocolate syrup, ½ teaspoon anise flavoring. Serve in demitasse with twist of lemon and spoonful of whipped cream. Serves 12.

SYRIAN

Put several crushed cardamom seeds in each demitasse. Pour in extra strong coffee. Serve with sugar.

VIENNESE

Brew extra strong coffee. Serve with or without hot milk and top with spoon of sweetened whipped cream.

WITH SPIRITS

CAFÉ BRÛLOT

Break up 2 sticks of cinnamon and combine in chafing dish with 10 whole cloves, 1 orange and 1 lemon peel each cut in one long strip, 12 lumps of sugar and 8 cups very strong hot coffee. Bring just to boil and carefully pour in 1½ cups brandy or cognac. Ignite brandy in a tablespoon held over surface. When flames subside, serve at once in standard cups or demitasse. Serves 8+.

CAFÉ DIABLE

In chafing dish combine and heat well 6 teaspoons sugar, 6 whole cloves, a 1-inch cinnamon stick, peels

of 1 lemon and 1 orange, cut in long strips, and 1½ cups strong hot coffee. Heat ¾ cup brandy in a cup, light and pour into hot coffee mix. Ladle into demitasse. Serves 4-5.

CAFÉ ROYALE

Over a cup of hot black coffee, hold a lump of sugar on a spoon. Pour an ounce of bourbon through lump into coffee and light sugar lump. When it has burned out, serve. Serves 2 demitasses.

COFFEE OLIO

Combine slivers of orange and lemon rind, 2 tablespoons sugar, 2 ounces brandy and 1 ounce each of Benedictine, rum, and kummel, whole cloves and cinnamon sticks to taste. Add 8 cups strong coffee and boil briefly. Serve demitasse with dollop of chilled whipped cream. Serves 10.

IRISH COFFEE

For each ⅔ cup strong hot coffee, add 1 teaspoon sugar and 3 tablespoons Irish whiskey. Top with whipped cream.

MINTED MUG

Pour 1 teaspoon chocolate syrup into warm mug and fill ¾ full with strong hot coffee. Top with scoop of vanilla ice cream and 1 jigger creme de menthe. Serves 1.

ROYAL MUG

Into heated mug pour ⅔ cup hot coffee, 1 tablespoon each of white creme de menthe and Kahlua and ½ teaspoon Drambuie. Top with whipped cream. Serves 1.

RUM MUG

Dissolve 1½ teaspoons sugar in 1 tablespoon hot coffee in mug. Add ¼ cup warm rum and fill mug with hot coffee, leaving enough room to float whipped cream on top. Serves 1.

SPANISH QUEIMADA

Fill earthenware bowl partly with brandy, zest with lemon peel, set ablaze and stir. Over this pour strong, heavily sweetened coffee. This extinguishes the flames and you dip your coffee cups into the brew.

And all this has been just the beginning of the ways you can enjoy coffee and its companions.

INDEX OF RECIPES

We acknowledge with thanks the following:

Gordian-Max Rieck GmbH, Hamburg for permission to reprint photographs and prints from COFFEA CURIOSA © 1968, published by Gordian-Max Rieck GmbH, Hamburg. pp. 0, 3, 6, 9, 16, 20, 50, 52

Rijksmuseum Netherlands Scheepvaart Museum Amsterdam. Flube Ship, Ca. 1630, p. 11

Niemeyer Nederlands Tabacologisch Museum, Groningen; Koffiebrevier © 1974, by Kurt Benesch: pp. 26, 31

Service de Documentation Photographique de la Réunion des Musées Nationaux, Paris. p. 14, top right

G. Michael Sellars, Paris. pp. 24, 39, 40, 42, 43, 47

Hills Bros. Coffee, San Francisco, p. 32

The Coffee and Tea Cabinet of Douwe Egberts Royal Tobacco Factories, Coffee Roasters & Tea Packers at Utrecht, Holland: pp. 19, 27, 55, 56, 57, 90, 101

Freed Teller & Freed Coffee and Tea, San Francisco: pp. 71, 72, 73

Graffeo Coffee House, San Francisco: pp. 75, 86

House of Coffee, San Francisco: pp. 84, 85

Simon Levelt b.v. Amsterdam; p. 87

M.J.B. Co., San Francisco: p. 104

All other photographs and all chart illustrations, Alan Wood, pp. 17, 76-81, 98, 99, 105-117.

OTHER BOOKS BY CHARLES & VIOLET SCHAFER
PUBLISHED BY TAYLOR & NG
HERBCRAFT
WOKCRAFT
EGGCRAFT
BREADCRAFT
TEACRAFT